NORTH KOREA'S PERPETUAL PROVOCATIONS: ANOTHER DANGEROUS, ESCALATORY NUCLEAR TEST

HEARING

BEFORE THE

SUBCOMMITTEE ON ASIA AND THE PACIFIC

OF THE

COMMITTEE ON FOREIGN AFFAIRS HOUSE OF REPRESENTATIVES

ONE HUNDRED FOURTEENTH CONGRESS

SECOND SESSION

—————

SEPTEMBER 14, 2016

—————

Serial No. 114–230

—————

Printed for the use of the Committee on Foreign Affairs

Available via the World Wide Web: http://www.foreignaffairs.house.gov/ or
http://www.gpo.gov/fdsys/

—————

U.S. GOVERNMENT PUBLISHING OFFICE

21–543PDF   WASHINGTON : 2016

For sale by the Superintendent of Documents, U.S. Government Publishing Office
Internet: bookstore.gpo.gov   Phone: toll free (866) 512–1800; DC area (202) 512–1800
Fax: (202) 512–2104   Mail: Stop IDCC, Washington, DC 20402–0001

CONTENTS

NORTH KOREA'S PERPETUAL PROVOCATIONS: ANOTHER DANGEROUS, ESCALATORY NUCLEAR TEST

WEDNESDAY, SEPTEMBER 14, 2016

HOUSE OF REPRESENTATIVES,
SUBCOMMITTEE ON ASIA AND THE PACIFIC,
COMMITTEE ON FOREIGN AFFAIRS,
Washington, DC.

The subcommittee met, pursuant to notice, at 3:27 p.m., in room 2255, Rayburn House Office Building, Hon. Matt Salmon (chairman of the subcommittee) presiding.

Mr. SALMON. I apologize for both of us being a little bit tardy. We had the Foreign Minister from Burma, who was here to meet with the chairman of the full committee, and we were asked to attend. So, thanks for being so patient. I really appreciate you not leaving.

The subcommittee will come to order. Members present will be permitted to submit written statements to be included in the official hearing record.

Without objection, the hearing record will remain open for 5 calendar days to allow statements, questions and extraneous materials for the record, subject to the length limitation in the rules.

Last Friday, North Korea conducted its fifth and most powerful nuclear test to date. This latest provocation coming just weeks after they fired off three additional missiles during the G-20 summit in China. While U.S. and United Nations sanctions have undoubtedly hurt the North Korean economy, Kim Jong-un continues to willingly and belligerently defy U.N. Security Council resolutions as well as international norms. Clearly, he is not fazed by the administration's so-called plan of strategic patience, and so continues with his childlike behavior that endangers much of the world. The House Committee on Foreign Affairs, under the leadership of Chairman Royce, has taken the lead to address this intransigence. While we have already taken bold steps in increasing sanctions, clearly, more must be done. We are here today to identify and work toward proactive policy solutions that will put an end to the provocations of this rogue regime. Enough is enough.

As good as the additional sanctions have been, without China's enforcement, it will never be enough. I would like to hear from our panel on how to best engage China on this issue. We have been talking about this for a very, very long time, and it doesn't seem like we have gotten them properly motivated. We have talked to

2

some of our allies about the same issue. And, frankly, China's almost nonintervention in this issue is very, very frustrating. We would love to hear any thoughts you might have on how we can get them a little bit more excited about getting more involved.

China prefers the status quo in North Korea rather than risk a flood of North Korean refugees and a shared border with the Korea-U.S. alliance. Some experts even worry that China may use its enforcement of U.N. Security Council resolutions and diplomatic assistance as a wedge, forcing South Korea to choose between China and the United States as its main partner on the peninsula. The international community at large is alarmed at China's indifference to date over North Korean provocations, especially with nuclear detonations so near its own border. Even North Korea's willingness to embarrass China by upstaging the G-20 ceremonies with a nuclear test has not yet led to real action by China.

The administration has appeared to make some progress on our trilateral engagement with Korea and Japan, our two closest allies in East Asia. The House recently passed my legislation, which was cosponsored by Mr. Sherman, to encourage further dialogue and cooperation between our nations, with particular emphasis toward the North Korean threat. I will be very interested to hear from our panel on the potential for further cooperation from South Korea and Japan on how we might best work together to address North Korea's dangerous behavior.

The United States recently convened its annual joint military exercises with South Korea. The U.S. flew two bombers over South Korea to provide some reassurance to our friends in Seoul, but I am not sure these messages resonate with Pyongyang. We all know that there are few options to instill real change from within North Korea, but waiting it out will not solve anything. We need a proactive approach.

Most agree that getting information to the people of North Korea, unfiltered by the current regime, would greatly benefit the people of North Korea and aid efforts to diminish the stranglehold Kim has over the nation. I have legislation that passed through this subcommittee that would provide an overdue update and enhancement of those efforts. Boosting the information flow in North Korea would cripple Kim Jong-un where he is most vulnerable, and that is in the realm of reality.

Again, sanctions efforts have been a huge focus in Congress, but due to China's lack of resolve, they seem to have little practical impact. I would like to determine what we can do to take it to the next level. What other chokepoints can we squeeze to shut off funding to North Korea's nuclear ambitions? Cutting off access to financial messaging systems, such as SWIFT, was a successful strategy to induce compliance with Iran, and we should pursue the same strategy toward North Korea, in my belief. The rogue regime should not have access to the international financial system.

As if its other activities weren't reason enough to cut off its financial messaging access, North Korea has been identified as the likely culprit of a serious hack on SWIFT earlier this year, in which the culprits stole $81 million from Bangladesh's central bank. For that reason, I am working on legislation to end North

Korea's access to interbank financial transfers to prevent further abuses and reduce funding to North Korea's nuclear program.

Time and again, North Korea has proven that, so long as it is able, it will continue to advance its nuclear program, for both internal domestic strength as well as international bargaining power. While the United States has shown a willingness to negotiate with North Korea when it takes even modest steps toward denuclearization, North Korea has shown no interest—zero interest—in maintaining international norms. This cycle cannot continue, and we cannot strategically wait with a potential catastrophe looming.

I look forward to a frank discussion with our witnesses on what to do next with this rogue regime.

And I would like to recognize the ranking member for his opening statement, and then we will go to you, the witnesses. Thank you.

Mr. SHERMAN. Mr. Chairman, thank you for holding these hearings. To amplify your reason why we were both late, we met with the Foreign Minister of Burma, also known as Myanmar, who happens to be Aung San Suu Kyi, one of the most inspirational women in the world. And, some would say, the de facto head of state of an important nation in Southeast Asia.

I want to thank you for holding these hearings as we look at North Korea's fifth test overall. Its second test conducted just this year. The bomb's yield is estimated to be as much as 20 kilotons or even more. And, if accurate, that would mean that the test involved a bomb with at least twice the yield of any other bomb tested by North Korea. We used to have the luxury of saying the North Koreans just want to get our attention; they just want some this or that concession. That is why they tested the missile; that is why they tested the nuclear explosive device. We can no longer just view North Korea as an annoying, petulant child. It is clear that North Korea is testing missiles and bombs for the purpose of developing warheads and ICBMs that can be put together and can reach our allies and, ultimately, the continental United States. The testing they are engaging in is necessary to achieve that goal. The fact that North Koreans have greatly increased the tempo of their testing is consistent with the view of an all-out effort to achieve these frightening capacities.

We need to approach this problem with both a clenched fist and an open hand. As to the clenched fist, we can have sanctions on North Korea and its leaders, but these will be significant but not enough to change its policy unless we have the cooperation of China. China is North Korea's lifeline, whether it is food, whether it is oil, whether it is trade, whether it is money, whether it is hard currency. China is North Korea's window to the world and the provider of the financial services that they need. China needs to realize that there will be consequences well beyond our current targeted sanctions on this or that business entity if it continues to do business as usual with North Korea. China needs to understand that if North Korea uses its nuclear weapons, we will blame not only the regime in Pyongyang but also the regime in Beijing. China needs to know that it risks a serious change in relationship with the United States if it does not assist us in this effort. It cannot assume that it will always have access to the United States market the way it does now. And, there are those who say that it is unthinkable to link the trading relationship with the foreign policy relationship. I think it is time to think the unthinkable. But, what we are likely to do is just keep doing what we have been doing, which has been very ineffective in stopping North Korea's efforts.

At the same time, we need an open hand. We should be discussing with North Korea a nonaggression pact, if they are still seeking one. We should be discussing with China that if there was a unification of the Korean Peninsula, something I don't think is going to happen anytime soon, but that if that were to happen, that the United States would not take military advantage of that, that, if anything, there would be a smaller American military presence on the Korean Peninsula and that it would not be north of the 38th parallel.

And, we should explore whether some of our sanctions on North Korea could be reduced or eliminated, at least for a while, if there were very intrusive inspections to enforce a regime that froze its nuclear program. The idea of accepting, even for a while, that North Korea keeps what it has may sound like a departure from orthodoxy. But, every year, they have more, and it would be a good year if they did not increase their nuclear capabilities.

I should point out that North Korean nuclear doctrine seems to call for having about 12 usable nuclear weapons to defend their country. They will soon have a 13th, and it may go on eBay. Not exactly on eBay, but once they get a certain number, they can think of selling the next one. If it is sold, it will not be for tens of millions of dollars; it will be for billions of dollars. Fortunately, there is no terrorist organization in the world that can provide that amount of money, but I can think of one or two states that would like to have nuclear weapons that could muster billions of dollars. And, I am going to continue my effort to convince the Chinese Government that they should not allow nonstop flights between Pyongyang and Tehran that don't stop for fuel in China. It is always good to get more fuel, and it is always good for the Chinese Government to be in a position to know what is on the plane.

What is more likely is we are just going to keep doing what we are doing. We will talk at China, but we won't do anything that forces them to change their policy. And we will be back here, unfortunately, without our chairman in the years to come—unless you want to do a third iteration of your congressional career to hold hearings—and by then, we may be talking about testing an ICBM that has proven to go thousands of miles. I don't want to be here to do that, but I am not moving to Arizona, so if it does happen, I will be here to see it.

And, I yield back.

Mr. SALMON. I thank you.

In the interest of time, we would like to move to the witnesses, and upon your conclusion, we will have questions by the members of the panel up here.

You have all testified before Congress before, but let me just remind you that, with our lighting system, when it is green, you are good as gold; when it turns amber, you have got a minute left;

when it is red, please finish. I know we have a lot of questions, a lot of interest. This is a very pressing issue and pressing time.

First of all, we have Dr. Cha, senior adviser and Korea chair at the Center for Strategic and International Studies; Mr. Bruce Klingner, senior research fellow for Northeast Asia at the Heritage Foundation; we have Dr. Sue Mi Terry, managing director of Bower Group Asia; and Mr. David Albright, the president and founder of Institute for Science and International Security.

We thank the panel for joining us today to share their experience and expertise.

And, Dr. Cha, we will start with you.

STATEMENT OF VICTOR CHA, PH.D., SENIOR ADVISER AND KOREA CHAIR, CENTER FOR STRATEGIC AND INTER-NATIONAL STUDIES

Mr. CHA. Thank you, Chairman Salmon, Representative Sherman, and committee members.

North Korea is shaping up to be the number one security threat for the next U.S. Presidency. Since 2009, there have been 62 ballistic missile and nuclear tests, versus 17 ballistic missile and nuclear tests during the Clinton and Bush administrations. So, there has been a steep change, and neither of the candidates have really addressed this issue. This issue is going to hatch in the next administration.

What the North Koreans want—as Representative Sherman said, we used to think they wanted attention and that is why they did these sorts of things. That is clearly not what we are talking about anymore. In my opinion, they are trying to demonstrate, to the best of their ability, a survivable nuclear capability. And, they are trying to do that, at least signal that, before the next U.S. President comes into office.

And I think we have more provocations to come. The data that we are collecting at CSIS on our Beyond Parallel Web site, which we will be releasing soon, indicates that they like to do things in a specified window around U.S. Presidential elections. So, I expect that there is more to come.

The threats are obvious, and I think both Chairman Salmon and Representative Sherman have spoken to these. And, I particularly want to emphasize the horizontal proliferation threat. I mean, their statements are talking about standardizing a weapons design. The suggestion is that the next step is production. And, if they do produce scores of missiles, nuclear-tipped missiles, there is only one thing that they can do with them, and that is to sell them. History has shown that they have sold every finished weapon system they have ever developed, whether it is missiles to Pakistan and Iran, whether it is a nuclear design for a 5-megawatt reactor to Syria, or even discussions with Saddam Hussein at one point, except Saddam was not ready to pay for anything yet.

Unfortunately, we are going to go back to the usual playbook: Angry statements from the United Nations, perhaps another Security Council resolution.

The sanctions are not doing the things that we want them to do. They are not retarding the program. They are not forcing the North Koreans back to the negotiation table. And they are not—even though this is an unspoken aspect of sanctions—they are not causing the regime to be unstable. So the current pattern is not working.

So, what should we do? I mean, I will offer some ideas. I don't know if they are new ideas, but I will offer some ideas. The first, and I think foremost, is that we need to deploy THAAD on the Korean Peninsula. Both the South Korean people and U.S. forces on the peninsula are naked without it. And, I know this is shaping up to be a controversial issue in South Korea, but this is not a political issue, even though it is being played as political in South Korea. This is a national security issue.

Second, I think we can do more in terms of sanctions. We can certainly boost or turbocharge the sanctions. We can close the loophole in 2270 when it comes to the sectoral measures, coal and these sorts of things. We can ban fuel exports to North Korea. We can ban the overseas labor exports. As Chairman Salmon said, we can do something with SWIFT. We can designate Air Koryo for violating the U.N. ban on importing luxury goods and bulk cash transportation. We can try to ban North Korean transactions in other foreign currencies, including the RMB. So there are a number of sanctions that we could do.

I also want to draw attention to the importance of continuing to focus on trying to implement the U.N. Commission of Inquiry recommendations, including discussion in the U.N. Security Council about holding North Korean leaders responsible for human rights abuses.

I do agree that we can't do all of this without leaving open some sort of diplomatic path. Otherwise, we are just headed on a path to war. And, so I think, in this regard, China should convene a five-party meeting. When we created the Six Party Talks, that was the purpose, was to have five-party meetings in which we could talk with the Chinese and others about more coordination on contingency planning.

Finally, let me say that I think we do need to engage China more on sanctioning, but I think we also need to engage them on thinking about the overall direction of the leadership in North Korea and how we might be able to effect change there. This problem, as we can see, based on the number of tests they have been doing, really coincides with the assumption of power of this leadership, this new young leadership. And, as long as that is there, this is going to continue to be a problem. Thank you very much.

[The prepared statement of Mr. Cha follows:]

CSIS | CENTER FOR STRATEGIC & INTERNATIONAL STUDIES

Statement before the

House Committee on Foreign Affairs

Subcommittee on Asia and the Pacific

"North Korea's Perpetual Provocations: Another Dangerous, Escalatory Nuclear Test"

A Testimony by:

Dr. Victor D. Cha

Professor of Government, Georgetown University

Senior Adviser and Korea Chair, Center for Strategic and

International Studies

and Fellow in Human Freedom, George W. Bush Institute

September 14, 2016

2255 Rayburn House Office Building

8

September 14, 2016

Chairman Salmon, Representative Sherman (ranking Democrat) and distinguished members of the committee, it is a distinct honor to appear before this committee to discuss the challenges posed by North Korea in the wake of its fifth nuclear test.

The #1 threat to the next U.S. presidency

North Korea's fifth nuclear test last week is the latest in a pattern of aggressive WMD provocations. According to CSIS *Beyond Parallel* Original Datasets, the nuclear detonation and the prior week's ballistic missile launches tally 62 provocations (see appendix A) since President Obama came to office.[1]

By any metric this represents a heightened tempo of activity. During the 1994-2008 period according to open source data, for example, the North conducted only 17 missile tests and one nuclear test (see appendix A). North Korea is the darkest stain on the Obama presidency's pivot to Asia, and will present itself as the most immediate national security threat to a Clinton or Trump presidency.

What do they want?

Testing was once interpreted by pundits to be an attention-getting effort for dialogue with the United States, and therefore was not appreciated for the face-value that the threat presented. Whether true or not in the past, it would be irresponsible today to adhere to such an interpretation.

North Korea is executing a strategy designed to demonstrate a survivable nuclear deterrent before the next U.S. administration comes into office. This means that further tests are likely if there are technological hurdles still not surmounted. Over the past year, Pyongyang, through propaganda photos and demonstrations, have signaled every element of a nuclear deterrent including a miniaturized warhead, re-entry vehicle, solid fuel propellant, and mobile-launch capabilities from sea and from land. CSIS *Beyond Parallel* datasets also indicate that additional demonstrations are likely in a defined time-window bracketing the U.S. presidential election in November.[2]

North Korean statements suggest the regime is ready to mass-produce nuclear-tipped ballistic missiles as they had "standardized" a design. While there is requisite bluster in every North Korean statement, and even though this adversary is still years away from striking the U.S. homeland with a ballistic missile, we must accept now that 1) they threaten U.S. troops in Korea and Japan, and as far away as Guam and Hawaii; and 2) they are well on a path to field an ICBM force to reach the U.S.

The goal, moreover, is not to produce a few bombs in the basement; instead, it is a force of 100 or more nuclear-armed weapons, ranging from long-range strike to battlefield use that could be employed in a shooting war.[3] North Korea's strategic goals are to deny the U.S. access to the region with a survivable nuclear threat, to break the extended deterrence guarantees in the alliance, and to eventually coerce South Korea into suing for peace. With the United States, the

---

1 Victor Cha, "Snapshot of North Korea's Five Nuclear Tests," Beyond Parallel, September 9, 2016, retrieved from http://beyondparallel.csis.org/fifth-nuclear-test-snapshot/
2 Victor Cha, "North Korean provocations and U.S. presidential elections," Beyond Parallel, http://beyondparallel.csis.org (forthcoming).
3 Jeffrey Lewis, "The Fifth Test: North Korea Building a Strategic Rocket Force?" *Beyond Parallel*, September 9, 2016, http://beyondparallel.csis.org/the-fifth-test-north-korea-building-a-strategic-rocket-force/

North seeks a peace treaty not so much to end the Korean war, but to codify U.S. recognition of it as a bona fide nuclear weapons state.

The media's focus on Pyongyang's drive to perfect a nuclear missile that can reach the United States obscures a second problem deriving from the program's development – horizontal proliferation. North Korea has sold every weapons system that it has ever developed. The Pakistani Ghauri missile is a North Korean missile. The Iranian Shahab missile is a North Korean missile.[4] The nuclear reactor building in Syria pre-emptively destroyed by the Israelis on September 6, 2007 showed designs identical to the 5-megawatt reactor in North Korea.[5] If North Korea starts to amass some version of its "standard" nuclear missile, there is no guarantee that they will not sell those weapons as they have sold past systems.

Ineffective responses

The international response to this strategy is as predictable as it is ineffective. The UN will respond with a statement of condemnation and possibly another Security Council resolution authorizing additional multilateral sanctions. The U.S. will likely move some assets to the region (Hawaii, Guam, and the Korean peninsula) to enhance deterrence posture, will encourage more U.S.-ROK-Japan trilateral military cooperation, and will implement more unilateral sanctions. The increasing proximity of North Korean recent missile projectiles within Japan's ADIZ will boost Prime Minister Shinzo Abe's plans for enhancing Japan's defense capabilities. In South Korea, the fifth test will lead Park to focus her remaining year in office almost exclusively on national defense, as evidenced by THAAD and step increases in defense spending for 2017.

Sanctions have become a reflexive response and political panacea for shelving the North Korean problem. Multilateral and unilateral measures imposed after North Korea's 4th nuclear test in January have yet to be fully implemented and assessed. However, initial indications are that short of China cutting off border trade, closing off airspace and ports, terminating energy assistance, and restricting North Korean access to the Chinese financial system, sanctions are largely failing to achieve any of the following three objectives: 1) they are not weakening the regime; 2) they are not coercing a return to the negotiating table; and 3) they are not retarding the growth of the program. The result is a perpetual punting of the issue from administration to administration.

China may undertake some initial sanctions unilaterally against the regime, as well as sign on to another UN Security Council resolution. But ultimately, these activities will be tempered by Beijing's net assessment that destabilizing Pyongyang is more incongruous with Chinese interests than a burgeoning nuclear program.

Road ahead

Any serious reassessment of policy must operate from certain assumptions. First, North Korea will continue on its nuclear path as dictated by the current leadership. Kim Jong-un is firmly in control of the country and he appears to have eliminated any elites in the military or party who might oppose his decisions. The lack of internal opposition, and Kim Jong-un's unwavering belief that a dual-track policy of economic development and nuclear weapons development will

[4] Paul K. Kerr et al., "Iran-North Korea-Syria Ballistic Missile and Nuclear Cooperation," CRS Report R43480, February 26, 2016, https://www.fas.org/sgp/crs/nuke/R43480.pdf; Larry Niksch, "The Iran-North Korea Strategic Relationship," Testimony before the House Committee on Foreign Affairs, July 28, 2015, 7-8, 16-17.
[5] Paul K. Kerr et al., "Iran-North Korea-Syria Ballistic Missile and Nuclear Cooperation," 6-7; [Nuclear Threat Initiative]. (2013, December 6). al-Kibar Plutonium Production Reactor – Syria. [Video File]. Retrieved from https://www.youtube.com/watch?v=kz6xVVMa2nM.

Cha: North Korea Testimony to HFAC Subcommittee on Asia   September 14, 2016

succeed (i.e. he can have his cake and eat it too), make it highly unlikely that North Korea will stop this nuclear inertia of its own accord. The increased tempo of testing, for example, which began in January 2009 does not just correspond with Obama's entrance to the White House. It also corresponds roughly with the period in which Kim Jong-un was designated the next future leader of North Korea.[6] Data suggests that under Kim Jong-un, North Korea's nuclear and missile testing will continue to increase in intensity and frequency to achieve the desired results.

Second, negotiations may serve the purpose of curtailing further testing and provocations, but they will not retard the growth of the program. With each missile and nuclear test, Kim Jong-un appears to be gaining confidence and certainty that the world will recognize North Korea as a nuclear state and deal with it on those terms. North Korea has refused to participate in denuclearization talks despite multiple offers. Pyongyang has instead countered with proposals for disarmament talks (and a peace treaty) which would require the U.S. and its allies to acknowledge North Korea as a nuclear weapons state. The measures taken by the members of the Six-Party Talks and the UN have yet to reverse Kim Jong-un's growing confidence in North Korea's asymmetrical military capabilities.

Third, absent a change in its strategic thinking, China will limit its cooperation to those measures that do not risk a collapse of the regime. Following the September 9th test, China was critical of North Korea but it also blamed the U.S. and South Korea for provoking Pyongyang through the deployment of THAAD on the Korean peninsula. China is clearly frustrated with North Korea, but given Beijing's strategic outlook it remains to be seen how much additional pressure they are willing to impose on their neighbor.

And fourth, the threat currently faced in the theater by North Korea's nuclear progress will enlarge to a homeland threat in the course of the next administration's tenure. Pyongyang's pursuit of a range of nuclear weapons and missile systems indicates that North Korea is intent on acquiring a nuclear-tipped ICBM capable of hitting the continental United States and also developing a second-strike nuclear capability to deter any preemptive military actions.

Where does this leave us? What does it mean if we accept North Korea as it is and not as we wish it to be? Inevitably we are forced to make a decision between two different evils. Due to North Korea's singular focus on developing nuclear weapons and our own failure to stop the country's progress, we are ultimately left with two policy choices at this point. The first is to pursue negotiations with North Korea that could freeze their nuclear program but would be unlikely to achieve complete, verifiable, and irreversible denuclearization. This would likely reduce the frequency of provocations (as further testing would be prohibited) but it would also inadvertently acknowledge North Korea as a nuclear weapons state. This would do irreparable damage to the Nuclear Nonproliferation Treaty (NPT) regime and would likely lead to a nuclear domino effect, as South Korea and Japan pushed to develop their own programs in response. The U.S. and South Korea would also lose much of their moral authority as global champions of nuclear nonproliferation and their leverage to ultimately pressure North Korea to denuclearize completely.

---

[6] Kim Jong-il reportedly had a debilitating stroke in August 2008. Rumors of the North Korean leader's bad health were rampant but actual facts related to his stroke and medical condition were confirmed publically by his French doctor in December 2008. Steven Erlanger, "Doctor Confirms Kim Jong-il Stroke," *New York Times*, Dec. 11, 2008, http://www.nytimes.com/2008/12/12/world/asia/12kim.html. According to government and media reports, Kim Jong-un was designated as the primary successor shortly afterward in early 2009. See David E. Sanger, Mark Mazzetti and Choe Sang-Hun, "North Korean Leader is Said to Pick a Son as Heir," *New York Times*, June 2, 2009; "Speculation Varies on Kim Jong-il's Successor," *Yonhap News*, January 22, 2009, http://english.yonhapnews.co.kr/northkorea/2009/01/22/62/0401000000AEN20090121007400325F.HTML

Cha: North Korea Testimony to HFAC Subcommittee on Asia   September 14, 2016

The second choice is to continue to ramp up extensive pressure on North Korea (economic, political, diplomatic, and social) so that top-down and the bottom-up change eventually forces the regime to recalculate and abandon its nuclear weapons program. The main problem with this choice is that it is highly dependent on China and Russia's participation in the application of pressure, and it is banking on the fact that North Korea will cave into pressure before it will develop a complete and diversified nuclear weapons program. It also guarantees that there will be more North Korean provocations—running the risk of triggering military conflict due to miscalculation, distrust, and fear among countries in the region. Which of these pathways is the lesser of two evils?

Experts who have worked on the North Korean nuclear issue for years know that pressure and dialogue are not mutually exclusive and both should be tools that are used to address the problem. What is perhaps most challenging is determining a strategy that mostly effectively brings all the levers of power (economic, diplomatic, military, and technology/information) to bear on this vexing problem to produce a different and better outcome. The following are my recommendations on next steps that can be taken.

The first order of business is to utilize the fifth test as a platform to ramp up additional sanctions on the regime. A campaign among UN member states to stop the import of North Korean "slave labor," could arrest millions of dollars of annual income to the regime. Cutting North Korea off from the access to the international financial system might complicate the regime's ability to finance proliferation. Mobilizing UN Security Council members to implement the recommendations of the Commission of Inquiry Report on human rights abuses would be another important measure, since North Korea's nuclear program is intertwined with its abuse of its citizens. Appropriating more funds to support the delivery of information about the outside world to North Korea citizens hungry for such news would preserve a basic human right. There is a legitimate question, as well, about whether a country like North Korea that has violated over five UNSCRs should be considered worthy of membership in core international institutions.

Learned analysts over the past week have been cited projecting two roads ahead in resolving the current crisis. One is a road to war with all of its attendant costs and risks. The other is acceptance of North Korea as a nuclear weapons state, and trying to minimize the damage of the new situation with maximum deterrence and defense capacities with our allies.

A broader and deeper conversation is in order between the United States and its allies first, and then with others in the region about addressing the source of the problem rather than the symptoms. Regime collapse is understandably a proposition too risky for most to contemplate given the many unknowns and the risks of all-out war. However, encouraging voices more secular in nature and less tied to a cult of personality regime may offer change without the costs of collapse. A future leadership does not necessarily need to have democratic inclinations, though that would be preferred, because that is not the reality in North Korea. Leadership is likely to come from the military, which is the only organized social institution in the country with instruments of force. Secular dictators making rational economic decisions throughout history has been the lesser evil than cult-of-personality leaderships.

Appendix A: North Korean Missile Launches and Nuclear Tests (1994-2016)

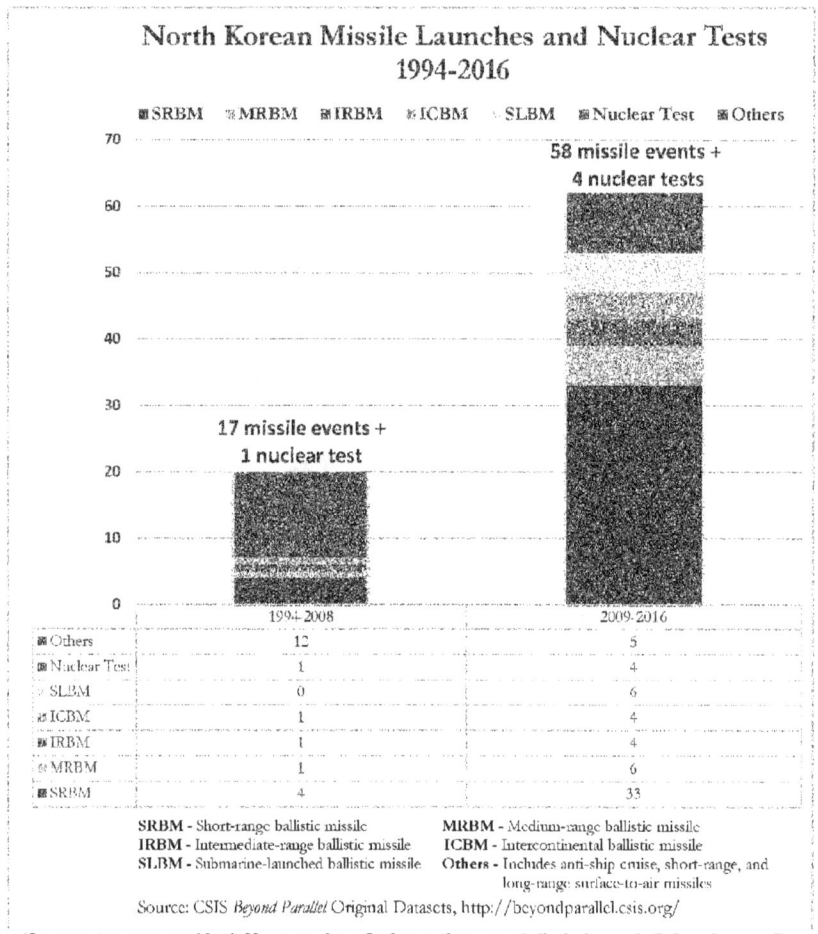

	1994-2008	2009-2016
Others	12	5
Nuclear Test	1	4
SLBM	0	6
ICBM	1	4
IRBM	1	4
MRBM	1	6
SRBM	4	33

SRBM - Short-range ballistic missile   **MRBM** - Medium-range ballistic missile
IRBM - Intermediate-range ballistic missile   **ICBM** - Intercontinental ballistic missile
SLBM - Submarine-launched ballistic missile   **Others** - Includes anti-ship cruise, short-range, and long-range surface-to-air missiles

Source: CSIS *Beyond Parallel* Original Datasets, http://beyondparallel.csis.org/

*In some circumstances, North Korea may have fired more than one missile during a missile launch event. For example, on July 4, 2006, three types of missiles were launched on the same day, but was counted as one event.

CSIS | CENTER FOR STRATEGIC & INTERNATIONAL STUDIES | Korea Chair |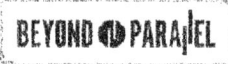

Mr. SALMON. Thank you.

Mr. Klingner.

STATEMENT OF MR. BRUCE KLINGNER, SENIOR RESEARCH FELLOW FOR NORTHEAST ASIA, THE HERITAGE FOUNDATION

Mr. KLINGNER. Thank you, Mr. Chairman, Ranking Member Sherman, and distinguished members of the panel. It is truly an honor to be asked to appear before you again on such an important issue to U.S. national security.

North Korea's repeated violations of U.N. resolutions have led to a new international consensus on the need for stronger, more comprehensive sanctions. The enhanced punitive measures are welcome, if long overdue, but their utility is dependent on complete and forceful implementation.

This year, Congress passed the North Korea Sanctions and Policy Enforcement Act, which had a major impact by inspiring or pressuring others to implement long overdue measures on North Korea. The act increased U.S. leverage at the U.N. Security Council. It led other nations to undertake similar actions or to wean themselves away from business dealings with Pyongyang. And it led the Obama administration to finally designate North Korea as a primary money laundering concern and target several North Korean entities, including Kim Jong-un, for human rights abuses. Yet, more can and needs to be done.

Besides the Obama administration's policy of timid incrementalism of sanctions enforcement, another major problem, as you have identified, is China. In March, China agreed to U.N. Resolution 2270, which has been touted as the toughest to date. That is true, but as has been the case with every previous resolution, it was watered down due to the demands of Beijing. And Chinese banks and businesses seemed to be pulling back from North Korea early in 2016. However, China took similar action after every previous North Korean nuclear test, and each time, China temporarily tightened trade and bank transactions with Pyongyang only to subsequently reduce enforcement and resume normal economic trade within only a few months. For years, China has been an enabler of North Korean misbehavior at the U.N.

China's reluctance to strongly pressure its ally provides Pyongyang a feeling of impunity, which encourages it only toward further belligerence. The effectiveness of international sanctions is hindered by China's weak implementation.

The economic noose is now tightening on the North Korean regime, and it faces a perfect storm of conditions that make it more vulnerable to economic pressure. The regime is facing a reduced flow of hard currency due to the increased financial sanctions; the increasing pariah status of the regime that is scaring away business partners; decreased global prices for resource commodities, which is a major North Korean export; the slowing Chinese economy; and South Korea ending its involvement in the failed Kaesong joint economic venture, which had generated nearly a quarter of North Korea's foreign trade.

Now, how to respond to North Korea? The international community should take all possible measures to cut off the flow of money into North Korea and substantially increase pressure on the re-

14

gime. In my written testimony, I have provided a lengthy list of specific recommendations, and I will highlight a few here.

There are additional measures we can take, but as important is fully implementing all the measures and the powers that we already have. But some of the steps, as you have already alluded to, are imposing secondary sanctions and penalizing entities, particularly Chinese financial institutions and businesses that trade with those on the sanctions list. Imposing secondary sanctions could have a chilling effect on Chinese economic engagement with North Korea. To date, the Obama administration has not sanctioned a single Chinese entity for facilitating North Korean prohibited behavior.

Compel the removal of North Korea from the SWIFT financial transfer network, as you pointed out, Mr. Chairman. The Obama administration and the European Union pressured the Belgian-based hub for electronic financial transactions to disconnect sanctioned Iranian banks in 2012. We should do the same with North Korea.

We should also work to ban North Korean overseas workers exploited in highly abusive conditions. North Korea has an estimated 60,000 to 100,000 workers overseas, earning the regime an estimated $300 million to $400 million a year. We should also increase information operations, through overt and covert means, to promote greater North Korean exposure to the outside world to have a long-term corrosive effect on the regime.

The U.S. and its allies must also implement measures to defend themselves against the spectrum of North Korea's military threat. As Mr. Cha has pointed out, we should deploy the THAAD ballistic missile defense system in South Korea. It is better than anything Korea has or will have for decades to defend against North Korean land-based missiles. We should also urge South Korea to deploy sea-based ballistic missile defense against the submarine missile threat from North Korea. Currently, Seoul has no systems to defend itself against an SLBM. We should also augment allied anti-submarine warfare capabilities. North Korea's apparent ability to evade allied submarine detection systems is worrisome.

And, finally, we should fully fund U.S. defense requirements. The U.S. military is smaller today than it was on 9/11.

In conclusion, at present, any offer of economic inducements to entice North Korea to abandon its nuclear arsenal is an ill-conceived Wile E. Coyote plan with little chance of success. Sanctions and targeted financial measures may take time to have an impact on the regime's financial condition. In the near term, however, such measures enforce U.S. and international law, impose a penalty on violators, and constrain the inflow and export of prohibited items for the nuclear missile programs. The difficulty will be maintaining international resolve to stay the course.

Thank you very much.

[The prepared statement of Mr. Klingner follows:]

The Heritage Foundation

CONGRESSIONAL TESTIMONY

Creating a Comprehensive Policy Response to

North Korean Threats and Provocations

Testimony before
House Committee on Foreign Affairs

Subcommittee on Asia and the Pacific of the

September14, 2016

North Korea's Perpetual Provocations:

Another Dangerous, Escalatory Nuclear Test

Bruce Klingner
Senior Research Fellow, Northeast Asia
The Heritage Foundation

Creating a Comprehensive Policy Response to
North Korean Threats and Provocations
Bruce Klingner

My name is Bruce Klingner. I am the Senior Research Fellow for Northeast Asia at The Heritage Foundation. The views I express in this testimony are my own, and should not be construed as representing any official position of The Heritage Foundation.

North Korea's repeated violations of U.N. resolutions have led to a new international consensus on the need for stronger, more comprehensive sanctions. The U.N., the European Union, the United States, and other countries have begun to implement stronger punitive measures to enforce laws, curtail proliferation, and raise the cost for Pyongyang's defiance of the international community.

This new consensus was triggered by cumulative anger and frustration from repeated North Korean violations, the realization that diplomatic engagement with Pyongyang was no longer a viable solution, heightened concern over North Korea's growing nuclear and missile threats, and a greater willingness to push China for more extensive sanctions.

The enhanced punitive measures are welcome, if long overdue, to sharpen North Korea's choice between its nuclear program and economic isolation. That all of these measures could have been implemented years ago is testament to a collective lethargy to confront North Korean belligerence. While new U.N. and U.S. sanctions are commendable, their utility is dependent on complete and forceful implementation.

Escalating North Korean Military Threat
During Kim's four-year reign, Pyongyang has conducted more than twice as many missile tests as his father Kim Jong-il did in 17 years in office. In 2016, North Korea has engaged in a rapid-fire series of nuclear and missiles tests, significantly augmenting and refining the nuclear threat to the United States and allies South Korea and Japan.

This year, Pyongyang successfully conducted two nuclear tests, an intercontinental ballistic missile test, breakthrough successes with its road-mobile intermediate-range missile and submarine-launched ballistic missile, re-entry vehicle technology, a new solid-fuel rocket engine, and an improved liquid-fuel ICBM engine.

In June, North Korea successfully tested a Musudan intermediate-range missile, leading experts to conclude the regime now has the ability to threaten U.S. bases in Guam, a critical node in allied plans for defending South Korea.

In July and August, No Dong medium-range missile tests were accompanied by North Korean statements that they were practice drills for preemptive nuclear attacks on South Korea and U.S. forces based there. A North Korean media-released photo showed the missile range would encompass all of South Korea, including the port of Busan where U.S. reinforcement forces would land.

A similar test in March was described by the regime as simulating a nuclear missile attack on South Korean targets conducted under "the simulated conditions of exploding nuclear warheads from the preset altitude above targets in the ports under the enemy control where foreign aggressor forces are involved."

Adm. Bill Gortney, commander of North American Aerospace Defense Command, assessed that North Korea is capable of putting a nuclear warhead on the No Dong medium-range ballistic missile that can reach all of South Korea and Japan.

Targeting the U.S. Homeland. In February, North Korea used a Taepo Dong (Unha) missile to put a satellite into orbit, the same technology needed to launch an ICBM nuclear warhead. Assessments indicate that the satellite was approximately 450 pounds, twice as heavy a payload as the previous successful satellite launch in Dec. 2012, and that the missile may have a range of 13,000 km, putting the entire continental United States within range.

Submarine Missile Threat. In August, North Korea conducted its most successful test launch of a submarine-launched ballistic missile which traveled 500 kilometers (300 miles). South Korean military officials reported that the missile was flown at an unusual 500-km high trajectory. If launched on a regular 150-km high trajectory, the submarine-launched missile might have traveled over 1,000 km.

Some South Korean military authorities warn deployment potentially could occur within a year. South Korea does not currently have defenses against submarine-launched ballistic missiles. The SM-2 missile currently deployed on South Korean destroyers only provides protection against anti-ship missiles. South Korea has recently expressed interest in the U.S.-developed SM-3 or SM-6 ship-borne systems to provide anti-submarine launched missile defense.

Some experts are dismissive of a submarine-based ballistic missile threat based on the perception that North Korea's old and noisy submarines would be easy to detect. However, in 2010, a North Korean submarine sank the South Korean naval corvette *Cheonan* in South Korean waters. In August 2015, 50 North Korean submarines—70 percent of the fleet—left port and disappeared despite allied monitoring efforts.

Despite post-*Cheonan* efforts, South Korean anti-submarine warfare capabilities remain an area of concern for allied military planners. A strong anti-submarine capability is not only critical for homeland defense but also for protecting sea lines of communication during a crisis on the Korean Peninsula.

U.N. Implements Stronger Sanctions
After nearly two months of debate, the U.N. Security Council unanimously approved Resolution 2270 in March 2016 to augment previous efforts to punish North Korea for its violations of U.N. resolutions. The tougher resolution reflected growing international concern over Pyongyang's growing nuclear capabilities and resolve to confront the regime's defiance.

The resolution went beyond previous U.N. actions by increasing financial sanctions, expanding required inspections of North Korean cargo, and targeting key exports. The resolution was the first instance of the U.N. targeting North Korean commercial trade, including mineral exports. The

18

sanctions and mandatory inspections of all cargo shipments will make foreign companies and investors more reluctant to engage with North Korea for fear of facing sanctions themselves.

Important Financial Provisions. A significant though easily overlooked provision is banning all financial institutions from initiating or maintaining a correspondent account with North Korea unless it is approved by the U.N. 1718 committee. Previously, the U.N. requirement was to prohibit correspondent accounts only if reasonable grounds exist for believing that they could contribute to North Korean nuclear or missile programs. If fully implemented, this new requirement could force disclosure of and increase scrutiny of all North Korean financial transactions.

Given international financial institutions' extreme sensitivity to reputational risk, this clause could also lead to increased due diligence efforts to prevent being even unwittingly complicit in North Korean illicit activities or cancelation of links with North Korea.

In 2005, the U.S. declared Macau-based Banco Delta a "money laundering concern," which, accompanied by *sub rosa* meetings by U.S. officials throughout Asia, led 24 financial institutions to sever relations with Pyongyang.

The new U.N. resolution is also notable for requiring mandatory inspections of *all* North Korean cargo transiting a country rather than only those suspected of carrying prohibited items. U.S. ambassador to the U.N. Samantha Power declared that all "cargo going into and coming out of North Korea will be treated as suspicious, and countries will be required to inspect it, whether it goes by air, land, or sea."

The resolution was passed with U.N. Charter Chapter 7, Article 41 authority rather than Article 42 (which allows for enforcement by military means). Article 42 authority would have enabled naval ships to intercept, board, and inspect North Korean ships suspected of transporting precluded nuclear, missile, and conventional arms, components, or technology.

Resolution 2270 is yet another attempt by the U.N. to punish North Korea for its blatant and repeated violations. However, U.N. members, most notably China, have been lackadaisical in enforcing previous resolutions. Although an improvement over its predecessors, in order for Resolution 2270 to effectively curtail North Korea's persistent violations, U.N. members need to take forceful and purposive steps toward enforcing the sanctions.

Congress Pushes for Stronger U.S. Actions
For years, the Obama Administration has been hitting the snooze bar on North Korean sanctions by not fully enforcing existing U.S. laws and regulations. Rather than fully utilizing existing authorities to target North Korean violators, the Obama Administration had pulled its punches. For example, the Obama Administration has still failed to sanction any Chinese entities for facilitating prohibited North Korean activity. Overall, the U.S. sanctions approximately the same number of North Korean entities as from Zimbabwe.

In February 2016, Congress, frustrated by the Administration's policy of timid incrementalism, stepped in to force the President to use the powers he already had to punish North Korea as well as Congress overwhelmingly approved the North Korea Sanctions and Policy Enhancement Act by Senate and House of Representatives votes of 96–0 and 408–2, respectively. The Act stands as an example of the kind of supra-partisan, supra-ideological unity needed to respond to North Korea's constant violations of U.N. resolutions, U.S. and international law, and the norms of international behavior.

That the North Korea Sanctions and Policy Enhancement Act (NKSPEA) makes enforcement of certain sections of U.S. laws *mandatory* rather than discretionary is a rebuke to Obama's minimalist approach. Although the introduction of new sanctions is vital, fully implementing and enforcing already existing far-reaching measures is of prime importance.

The Obama administration's designation in June of North Korea as a primary money laundering concern was likely brought on by Section 201 of the NKSPEA which "urge[d] the President, in the strongest terms—to immediately designate North Korea as a jurisdiction of primary money laundering concern" and imposed a requirement on the Secretary of Treasury to determine within 180 days whether "reasonable grounds exist for concluding that North Korea is a jurisdiction of primary money laundering concern."

Similarly, the administration's belated imposition in July of human rights-related sanctions was likely triggered by Section 304 of the NKSPEA which required the secretary of state to produce a report identifying North Korean entities "responsible for serious human rights abuses or censorship [and] make specific findings with respect to the responsibility of Kim Jong Un and of each individual who is a member of the National Defense Commission or the Organization and Guidance Department of the Workers' Party of Korea, for serious human rights abuses and censorship."

Chinese Policy Toward North Korea: Mix of Sanctions and Support
Faced with a stronger international consensus for greater pressure on North Korea, the Chinese government, as well as Chinese banks and businesses, undertook a number of promising actions early in 2016. Beijing accepted stronger text and sanctions in U.N. Resolution 2270 that went beyond previous U.N. resolutions. Chinese banks and businesses reduced their economic interaction with North Korea, though it is unclear whether it was due to government direction or anxieties over their own exposure to sanctions.

China Applies Pressure, But Gently. However, Beijing took similar action after each previous North Korean nuclear test. Each time, China temporarily tightened trade and bank transactions with Pyongyang and reluctantly acquiesced to incrementally stronger U.N. resolutions, only to subsequently reduce enforcement and resume normal economic trade with North Korea within months.

Oil Deliveries[1]

---

[1] For more detail and full citing, please see Bruce Klingner, "Chinese Foot-dragging on North Korea Thwarts U.S. Security Interests," The Heritage Foundation, August 11, 2016, http://www.heritage.org/research/reports/2016/08/chinese-foot-dragging-on-north-korea-thwarts-us-security-interests.

- **August–September 2006.** China reduced a "significant amount" of its oil supplies to North Korea following the July 2006 long-range missile launch and exported no crude oil to North Korea in September 2006.
- **October 2006.** China resumed exports of crude oil to North Korea in October, according to Chinese customs figures. Chinese oil shipments to North Korea in October were up 67 percent from a year earlier, despite the October 2006 nuclear test.
- **2009.** China reportedly suspended exports of crude oil for four months. However, there were no accompanying indications of oil shortages in North Korea, suggesting China had only pretended to cut off deliveries.
- **2011–2013.** China did not export any crude oil to North Korea in February 2011, February 2012, and February 2013. However, China often does not ship oil to North Korea in February because of seasonal factors. Since 2000, China shipped crude to North Korea in February only during 2001, 2004, 2009, and 2010. Annual Chinese shipments to North Korea in March are often double the usual amount, indicating the reason is not because of Chinese displeasure with nuclear or missile tests.
- **2014–2015.** Chinese customs statistics reported *no* Chinese oil exports to North Korea in 2014 or 2015. However, Chinese Ministry of Public Security officials commented, "We are continuously supplying oil" to North Korea. The deliveries are not recorded in Chinese customs data or foreign trade statistics because they are characterized as aid. Continued operations at North Korean refineries and stable petroleum prices indicated Beijing continued to provide 500,000 tons of oil annually. South Korean intelligence officials commented that China was secretly providing North Korea with oil.

Financial Transactions
- **2013.** China ceased financial transactions with North Korea's Foreign Trading Bank. The U.S. and South Korea had found dozens of accounts linked to Kim Jong-un in several banks in Shanghai and elsewhere in China. Beijing refused to allow them to be included in U.N. financial sanctions passed after North Korea's February 2013 nuclear test.
- **2016.** According to the U.N. Panel of Experts, North Korea used a Chinese bank to evade nuclear sanctions. The U.N. determined that Pyongyang transferred tens of millions of dollars through Bank of China's Singaporean branch. Chinese representatives at the U.N. delayed publication of the report as they previously hindered reports of Chinese noncompliance or malfeasance.

Bilateral Trade
- **October 2006.** The Chinese customs office in Dandong closed for 40 days. Approximately 80 percent of Chinese exports to North Korea pass through Dandong.
- **2007.** Chinese–North Korean trade rose 21 percent year-on-year during the several months following the October 2006 nuclear test.
- **2009.** Chinese authorities banned shipments of all metals and chemicals to North Korea that could be diverted to military use and issued a stern warning that it would severely punish any violating Chinese business. Beijing also began shutting off food exports to North Korea, allowing only shipments under 50 pounds for personal use.
- **2010.** After North Korea's 2009 nuclear test, Chinese trade and investment increased during the first 11 months of 2010 to $3 billion, a dramatic increase from $1.7 billion in 2009.
- **2013.** The Chinese Ministry of Transport directed customs agencies and logistics companies in Dandong and Dalian to strictly enforce U.N. Security Council Resolution 2087.

Concurrently, the Ministry of Finance began cracking down on illegal financial transactions by North Korean banks, including freezing North Korean assets.

- **2013.** According to Jilin Province officials, there were more stringent Chinese border checks and reduced bilateral trade for several weeks after North Korea's third nuclear test. The Chinese companies had reduced their exposure to North Korea due to concerns over the new sanctions but were assured by Beijing that they should continue business with North Korea as usual.
- **April 2013.** China increased border checks on trade shipments with North Korea. However, the flow of goods was largely unaffected, according to more than a dozen Chinese trading firms based near Dandong.
- **2015.** North Korean trade with China dropped nearly 15 percent in 2015 to $5.76 billion with North Korean export of coal and iron falling 6.3 percent and 68.5 percent, respectively. However, the downturn took place before North Korea's nuclear test, suggesting it could also be attributed to China's economic slowdown and Kim Jong-un's call for using homemade products.

China as Enabler of North Korean Misbehavior

In the U.N., China has acted as North Korea's defense lawyer by:
- Repeatedly resisting stronger sanctions;
- Watering down proposed resolution text;
- Insisting on expansive loopholes;
- Denying evidence of North Korea violations;
- Blocking North Korean entities from being put onto the sanctions list; and
- Minimally enforcing resolutions.

For example, while the latest U.N. resolution appears to ban export of key North Korean resource commodities such as coal and iron, China insisted on an exemption for "livelihood purposes." In implementing the U.N. resolution, Beijing simply requires any company importing North Korean resources to sign a letter pledging that it "does not involve the nuclear program or the ballistic missile program" of North Korea." The reality is that the loophole is larger than the ban, making the sanction largely ineffective.

Even after the latest U.N. resolution sanctions, China remains a reluctant partner, fearful that a resolute international response could trigger North Korean escalatory behavior or regime collapse. Beijing resists imposing conditionality in trade because it believes it could lead to instability and unforeseen, perhaps catastrophic, circumstances.

China's reluctance to strongly pressure its ally provides Pyongyang a feeling of impunity which encourages it toward further belligerence. North Korea is willing to directly challenge China's calls for peace, stability, and denuclearization by repeatedly upping the ante to achieve its objectives including buying time to further augment its nuclear and missile capabilities.

China's timidity, and the international community's willingness to accommodate it, only ensures continual repetition of the cycle with ever-increasing risk of escalation and potential catastrophe. The effectiveness of international sanctions is hindered by China's weak implementation.

Noose Tightening on North Korean Regime

North Korea faces a perfect storm of conditions that makes it more vulnerable to economic pressure. While sanctions only apply to prohibited activities, even legitimate North Korean enterprises are becoming less profitable. Increased financial sanctions, combined with the increasing pariah status of the regime, are reducing the flow of hard currency to the regime.

Diplomatic pressure, including on human rights violations and the abysmal conditions of North Korean overseas workers, is scaring away traders and drying up the regime's overseas sources of hard currency. North Korean diplomats are being deported, overseas workers are losing their visas, and countries are severing business contracts with the regime.

In an attempt to prevent further defections, North Korea recalled some trade officials, students, and workers from overseas which, in turn, further reduces the regime's ability to gain hard currency. Other factors constraining North Korea's economy include decreased world prices for resource commodities (a key North Korean export), the slowing Chinese economy, and South Korea ending its involvement in the joint Kaesong economic venture (which had generated 23% of North Korea's foreign trade).

The regime is now facing greater pressure amidst a deteriorating environment for recovery. Previously, some country or another was willing to step in to provide whatever support was necessary to prevent collapse. But, North Korean actions have reduced international community tolerance and created a new consensus for stronger sanctions.

Resorting to Desperate Measures. As a result of heightened UN sanctions on financial transactions, some North Korean trading companies have resorted to smuggling foreign currency into the country. North Korea appears to have resumed or reinvigorated its currency counterfeiting operations. Starting in March 2016, high quality counterfeit $100 bills were discovered in China with the North Korean government suspected as the source. The regime is also suspected in counterfeiting Chinese renminbi currency.

In February, North Korea conducted the first government-sponsored digital bank robbery. North Korean hackers gained access to the Society for Worldwide Interbank Financial Telecommunication (SWIFT) -- the system used by central banks to authorize monetary transfers – to send money transfer requests of $951 million from the Central Bank of Bangladesh to the New York Federal Reserve to transferred money to banks in the Philippines, Sri Lanka, and other parts of Asia.

The majority of the $951 million in fraudulent money orders was halted or recovered, but $81 million in transfers was laundered through casinos in the Philippines. Cyber security firms BAE Systems and Symantec identified North Korea as the most likely culprit. Both firms found links, including unique computer code, between the SWIFT hack and the 2014 hack of Sony Pictures by the North Korean affiliated hacker group Lazarus.

Time for Incrementalism Is Past

North Korea continues its relentless quest to augment and refine its nuclear weapons arsenal and missile delivery capabilities. Pyongyang's successful missile and nuclear tests show that it is only a matter of time before the regime will be able to threaten the United States directly with nuclear weapons. North Korea already threatens U.S. interests and allies in Asia.

The regime shows its disdain for international efforts to constrain its behavior by openly and repeatedly defying international law and U.N. resolutions. Responding with strong rhetoric and minimalist measures has only encouraged North Korea to remain on course.

The international community should take all possible measures do cut off the flow of foreign currency into North Korea. It should no longer hold some sanctions in abeyance, to be rolled out after the next North Korean violation or provocation. There will be little change until North Korea feels pain and China feels concern over the consequences of Pyongyang's actions and its own obstructionism.

The U.N. should:
- **Eliminate the "livelihood purposes" exemption** for North Korean export of its resources and impose a ban on sale of crude oil to North Korea.
- **Ban North Korea overseas workers exploited in highly abusive conditions.** Workers are stripped of their passports, denied most of their earnings, and forced to perform labor without compensation. North Korea has an estimated 60,000 to 100,000 overseas workers in 50 countries but mainly China and Russia, earning the regime an estimated $300 million to $400 million annually.
- **Target North Korean human rights violations which a U.N. Commission of Inquiry deemed "crimes against humanity."** Impose sanctions on North Korean entities, both at the individual and agency levels.

The United States should:
- **Impose secondary sanctions.** The U.S. should penalize entities, particularly Chinese financial institutions and businesses, that trade with those on the sanctions list or export prohibited items. The U.S. should also ban financial institutions that conduct business with North Korea from conducting business in the United States. Imposing secondary sanctions would have a chilling effect on Chinese economic engagement with North Korea since the risks would outweigh the economic benefits.
    - To date, the Obama Administration has not sanctioned a single Chinese entity for facilitating North Korean prohibited behavior. By hesitating to sanction Chinese violators due to concern of the impact on the strategic U.S.-Chinese relationship, the net effect is to give Chinese banks and businesses immunity from U.S. law.
- **Make clear to Beijing that Pyongyang is a national security threat to the U.S. and its allies** and that Chinese inaction or obstructionism on North Korea will impact the bilateral U.S.–China relationship.
- **Call on Beijing to abandon repatriation of North Korean defectors** and allow visits by the U.N. rapporteur on North Korean human rights to investigate refugee conditions in northeast China.

- **Compel the removal of North Korea from SWIFT financial transfers.** The Obama Administration and European Union pressured the Belgian-based Society for Worldwide

Interbank Financial Telecommunication (SWIFT) to disconnect sanctioned Iranian banks in 2012. The system is the world hub for electronic financial transactions.

- **Return North Korea to the state sponsors of terrorism list.** Inclusion on the list requires the U.S. government to oppose loans by international financial institutions, such as the World Bank, International Monetary Fund, and Asian Development Bank.
- **Increase information operations** to promote greater North Korean exposure to the outside world. Expand broadcasting services, such as by Radio Free Asia, and distribution of leaflets, DVDs, computer flash drives, documentaries, and movies into North Korea through both overt and covert means. Increased North Korean exposure to information is a useful long-term means to begin the transformation of the nature of the regime, as took place in Communist Eastern Europe and the Soviet Union.

Security-related

The U.S. and its allies must implement measures to defend themselves against the spectrum of North Korea's military threats.

- **Deploy the THAAD Ballistic Missile Defense System.** The Terminal High Altitude Area Defense (THAAD) is more capable than any system that South Korea has or would have for decades to defend against North Korean land-based missiles.
- **Refute fallacious Chinese arguments against THAAD.** Beijing asserted that THAAD deployment would impinge on its security interests. However, a careful analysis of THAAD interceptor and radar capabilities and Chinese missile deployment sites reveal Chinese technical objections are disingenuous.[2] Beijing's true objective is preventing improvement in allied defensive capabilities and multilateral cooperation.
- **Deploy sea-based ballistic missile defense against the submarine missile threat.** The THAAD system is not designed to counter SLBM threats. The X-band radar can only detect missiles in an approximate 90-degree arc, which would be directed toward North Korea, not the waters surrounding the Korean Peninsula. Therefore, Washington and Seoul should discuss deployment of SM-3 or SM-6 missiles on South Korean naval ships.
- **Augment allied anti-submarine warfare capabilities.** North Korea's apparent ability to evade allied submarine detection systems is worrisome. Washington should facilitate South Korean collection and analysis capabilities and linkage with U.S. naval intelligence. Seoul requires wide-area ocean-surveillance capability, for both coastal defense and blue-water operations.
- **Affirm U.S. resolve to support and defend our allies.** Ballistic missile defense is an important part of the broader strategy of strong alliances, forward-deployed U.S. military forces in the Pacific, and the extended deterrence guarantee.
- **Fully fund U.S. defense requirements.** The U.S. military is smaller today than it was on 9/11. The navy has 273 ships, 14% smaller than in 2001, and has not been this small since 1916. Five years ago the Army was building toward 48 brigade combat teams, today it has 32, a number that will likely drop to 24 or so by 2020. The Army will be smaller than at any time since 1940. The Air Force has 12 percent fewer personnel than on 9/11 and 26 percent fewer aircraft. In fact, the Air Force will have fewer planes than at any previous point in the

---

[2] Please see Bruce Klingner, "South Korea Needs THAAD Missile Defense," The Heritage Foundation, June 12, 2015, http://www.heritage.org/research/reports/2015/06/south-korea-needs-thaad-missile-defense.

history of the Air Force. The Marine Corps had 27 infantry battalions just a few years ago but is now on the way to 21.

Conclusion

At present, any offer of economic inducements to entice North Korea to abandon its nuclear arsenal is an ill-conceived plan with little chance of success. Instead, the consensus is that stronger sanctions must be imposed on North Korea for its serial violations of international agreements, U.N. resolutions, and U.S. law.

Washington must sharpen the choice for North Korea by raising the risk and cost for its actions as well as for those, particularly Beijing, who have been willing to facilitate the regime's prohibited programs and illicit activities and condone its human rights violations. Little change will occur until North Korea is effectively sanctioned, and China becomes concerned over the consequences of Pyongyang's actions and its own obstructionism.

Sanctions and targeted financial measures may take time to have an impact on the regime's financial condition. In the near-term, however, such measures enforce US and international law, impose a penalty on violators, and constrain the inflow and export of prohibited items for the nuclear and missile programs.

The difficulty will be maintaining international resolve to stay the course. Already, some have expressed impatience with the months-old sanctions and advocated a return to the decades-long attempts at diplomacy which failed to achieve denuclearization.

26

* * * * * * * * * * * * * * * * * * *

The Heritage Foundation is a public policy, research, and educational organization recognized as exempt under section 501(c)(3) of the Internal Revenue Code. It is privately supported and receives no funds from any government at any level, nor does it perform any government or other contract work.

The Heritage Foundation is the most broadly supported think tank in the United States. During 2014, it had hundreds of thousands of individual, foundation, and corporate supporters representing every state in the U.S. Its 2014 income came from the following sources:

Individuals 75%
Foundations 12%
Corporations 3%
Program revenue and other income 10%

The top five corporate givers provided The Heritage Foundation with 2% of its 2014 income. The Heritage Foundation's books are audited annually by the national accounting firm of RSM US, LLP.

Members of The Heritage Foundation staff testify as individuals discussing their own independent research. The views expressed are their own and do not reflect an institutional position for The Heritage Foundation or its board of trustees.

Mr. SALMON. Thank you.
Dr. Terry.

STATEMENT OF SUE MI TERRY, PH.D., MANAGING DIRECTOR, BOWER GROUP ASIA

Ms. TERRY. Mr. Chairman, Ranking Member Sherman, and distinguished members of the committee, thank you for this opportunity to testify before you on this very difficult problem.

North Korea is a very personal issue for me. My entire paternal side of the family came from the north, and I have personally witnessed the pain of divided families.

In the aftermath of the fifth nuclear test, again, the community of Korea watchers is divided as to what the next steps should be. As a number of North Korea experts argue, sanction strategy as a policy of U.S. policy is no longer working, and it is time to return to negotiations with North Korea even without preconditions. Other experts call for ratcheting up more pressure against the Kim regime by enforcement of sanctions and other measures, such as information warfare, even if it means potentially risking escalation by the regime or even potentially risking instability.

I actually believe that if there is any chance at all that North Korea would ever entertain the idea of ever giving up nuclear weapons program, it would be only because we have made it so that the Kim regime is facing a very stark choice between keeping its nuclear arsenal and regime survival.

Victor and Bruce Klingner just laid out before you—as they laid out, I agree that this ratcheting up pressure must begin with tougher sanctions and, more importantly, better enforcement. As you have heard, we have just not done that yet. It is premature to argue that sanctions are not working, or it has failed. Until February of this year, we did not even have comprehensive sanctions against North Korea. We finally have stronger sanctions in place, but for sanctions to work, it needs to be enforced.

Here again, the chief problem has been China. China is still reluctant to enforce—to implement the U.N. sanctions. There are many examples of China's noncompliance, and I point out some of this in my written testimony.

President Obama has also yet to fully use the broad powers that the Congress has given him to penalize any Chinese companies or banks for continuing to do business with North Korea. Confronting Kim Jong-un credibly depends on getting bankers in China and other countries to comply with the sanctions, which means a credible threat of secondary sanctions is necessary.

In addition to enforcement of sanctions, the next steps are to close existing loopholes and add even more individuals and entities to the list. You have heard what some of them could be both by Victor and Bruce. That includes banning labor and disconnecting North Korean banks from SWIFT system.

Beyond sanctions, I think there are other actions that we can take to ratchet up pressure, including: Promoting human rights in North Korea, seeking ways to increase information dissemination into the north, and finding ways to give Internet access to North Korean citizens. North Korea should also be placed back on the

State Sponsors of Terrorism list. I know you have discussed this with both speakers in the past.

Now, even as we push for enforcement of sanctions and ratcheting up pressure on the Kim regime, I am very aware that these measures could also fail and no amount of pressure may change the regime's calculus. Nonetheless, after more than two decades of dealing with North Korea, I think we are left with very, very few options. And if we manage to enforce sanctions, including secondary sanctions, over a sustained period of time, I think this will be the first time we decisively raised the stakes, the cost for Kim Jong-un in pursuing the nuclear weapons program. And this might, just might, make him reconsider his policies. If it doesn't and the critics of sanctions policy are right, that even the strictest enforcement of sanctions will not make the Kim regime reconsider its nuclear program. Even so, I believe enforcement of sanctions and a containment policy are the right next steps, even as we leave the door open for engagement down the road. In addition to sending a message to other rogue regimes about the cost of flouting international law, I think these pressures could also weaken Kim Jon-un's grip on power. And while they might at some point precipitate instability, potential instability, I believe that this is an outcome that we should welcome, not fear, because over the longer term, we should really be pursuing a policy of unification of the two Koreas.

Let me just conclude with this point. While Kim Jong-un's hold on power appears to be firm right now, I think there is a growing sign of discord among the elite class. We have recently seen an increasing rate of defection by very high-ranking elites. All these frequent purges and executions of high-level elites may help strengthen Kim Jon-un's rule in the short run, but all this heavy-handed rule is more likely to corrode long-term elite support for Kim.

This is, again, where the sanctions enforcement will help. The more we intensify economic pressure against the Kim regime, the more we shake the confidence of the elites, the more that Kim Jong-un will be left vulnerable, as he will have less foreign currency to underwrite the lifestyle of the elites, whose support is essential in maintaining his grip on power. And at the end of the day, it is when Kim Jong-un is facing really an abyss, he might finally choose to disarm, or, failing that, it may be that the North's policy will only change if a different leadership fundamentally emerged. Tightening the sanctions screws now, I think, will hasten that day. Thank you.

[The prepared statement of Ms. Terry follows:]

Statement before the

House Committee on Foreign Affairs

Subcommittee on Asia and the Pacific

"North Korea's Perpetual Provocations: Another Dangerous, Escalatory Nuclear Test"

A Testimony by:

Dr. Sue Mi Terry

Managing Director, Korea

Bower Group Asia

September 14, 2016

Chairman Salmon, Representative Sherman, and distinguished members of the Committee:

Thank you for the opportunity to testify before you today on the U.S. response to the North Korean threat.

North Korea's fifth nuclear test conducted on September 9th—the second this year alone—follows the test of a submarine-launched ballistic missile in early August. These tests show that North's nuclear arsenal and capability are developing at an alarming rate. While we can't confirm the North's claim that it has mastered the ability to mount miniaturized warheads capable of fitting on a ballistic missile that can reach the U.S. homeland, the test was nonetheless the strongest to date. The device that was tested on Friday reportedly yielded 20 to 30 kilotons, a much more powerful blast than North Korea's 7 to 9 kiloton detonation in January. Pyongyang issued a statement that it had tested a "nuclear warhead that has been standardized to be mounted on a strategic ballistic rockets of the Hwasong artillery units of the Strategic Forces of the Korean People's Army." By using the word "standardized," Kim Jong-un likely intended to convey that the North is able to produce nuclear warheads to arm missile force in quantity using various fissile materials. It shows Pyongyang's progress toward nuclear warhead miniaturization, directly threatening the United States.

What should be our response? All three U.S. administrations going back to the Bill Clinton presidency in the early 1990s have tried to address the North Korean threat through various means including negotiations sweetened by economic aid to Pyongyang. The North Koreans have been happy to pocket the aid, but they haven't delivered on their promises of ending their nuclear program. Far from moderating, the Kim Jong-un regime has accelerated the pace of the missile and nuclear program under his watch, and has been more brutal and unpredictable than ever, more so than even his father, Kim Jong-il.

In response to the growing North Korean threat, the community of Korea watchers is deeply divided as to what the next steps should be. In the aftermath of the fifth nuclear test, a number of Korea experts argue that the sanctions strategy has failed as an instrument of U.S. policy and it's time to return to diplomacy and negotiations with North Korea, even without preconditions. Other experts call for ratcheting up even more pressure on the Kim regime through sanctions enforcement and other measures such as information warfare, even if it means risking escalation by the North or even potential regime instability.

I believe returning to the talks now with the North by dropping preconditions will not yield the result we seek, which is denuclearization by the North. As we've seen with Burma, Iran, and Cuba, the Obama administration is not opposed to holding talks or negotiations with its adversaries. But the timing is not right to ease sanctions and return to dialogue with the North, particularly since the Kim regime itself has repeatedly said that it is no longer interested in denuclearization talks. In fact, the Kim regime has stressed in the past few years that it has no intention of ever giving up its nuclear arsenal, even revising its constitution to enshrine itself as a nuclear weapons state.   The North sees possessing nuclear weapons as essential for its national identity and security and for achieving power and prestige on the international stage. If there is any chance at all that the North would ever entertain the idea of giving up its nuclear program—which is, admittedly, only a remote possibility—it would be only because we have made it so that the Kim regime is facing a stark choice between keeping the nuclear arsenal and regime survival.

Tougher Sanctions, Better Enforcement

We have not yet done that. It is premature to argue that sanctions against North Korea have failed. It is important to remember that until February of this year, the U.S. did not maintain comprehensive sanctions against North Korea. As many North Korea sanctions experts like Joshua Stanton and Bruce Klinger have extensively written about and former U.S. government officials like Kurt Campbell have pointed out, the argument that North Korea sanctions have maxed out was simply untrue. Until this year, U.S. sanctions against North Korea were a mere shadow of the sanctions applied to Iran, Syria, or Burma, and even narrower than those applicable to countries like Belarus and Zimbabwe.[1]

Today, we finally have stronger sanctions in place for North Korea ever since the President has signed into law the North Korea Sanctions and Policy Enforcement Act in February, which gave him expansive new powers. The following month, in March, the United Nations Security Council also unanimously passed a resolution, United Nations Security Council Resolution 2270, imposing new sanctions on the Kim regime, including mining exports.   Moreover, triggered by requirements of the Sanctions Act, in June, the Obama administration finally designated North Korea as a primary money laundering concern, and in July, the Treasury Department designated Kim Jong-un and ten other senior North Korean individuals and five organizations for human rights violations.

For sanctions to work, however, they will need to be pursued over the course of several years, not a mere six months, and most importantly, they need to be enforced.   Here, our chief problem has been that China is still reluctant to follow through in fully and aggressively implementing the UN sanctions. There are many examples of China's non-compliance. For example, under UN Security Council Resolution 2270, all UN member states are required to inspect all cargo coming in

---

[1]See Joshua Stanton, "North Korea: The Myth of Maxed-Out Sanctions," *Fletcher Security Review*, Vol.2, No.1, January 21, 2015; Joshua Stanton, "Sanctions Worked Against North Korea, and They Can Work Again," *The Weekly Standard*, January 29, 2016; Joshua Stanton and Sung Yoon Lee, "Financial Could Force Reforms in North Korea," *The Washington Post*, February 20, 2014; Bruce Klinger, "Six Myths About North Korea Sanctions," CSIS Korea Chair Platform, December 19, 2014.

and out of North Korea, but there is a new report showing that China is essentially ignoring this requirement. Trucks are reportedly constantly traveling from China to North Korea to deliver goods and there appears to be little evidence customs agents are checking trucks as required.[2] Sanctioned North Koreans also have been seen leaving Chinese ports, and China continues to buy banned minerals like gold from the North, while continuing to import coal and iron from the North, trade which is supposed to be limited to "livelihood" purposes.[3] *Washington Post* reporter Anna Fifield reported in August that Chinese customs data showed that its trade with North Korea as of June this year was valued at $504 million, almost 10 percent higher than the previous year, in spite of three months of sanctions in place.[4]

President Obama has yet to use the broad powers that Congress gave him to make China pay a cost for this support of North Korea. He is yet to penalize any Chinese companies or banks for continuing to do business with the Kim regime. Confronting Kim Jong-un credibly depends on getting his bankers in China, Russia, Europe, and other places to comply with the sanctions, which means a credible threat of secondary sanctions is necessary on the part of the U.S. Section 104 of the North Korea Sanctions and Policy Enhancement Act imposes severe and mandatory sanctions in order to target the slush funds that facilitate Kim Jong-un's proliferation, arms trafficking, cyber attacks, the trade in certain minerals, luxury goods imports, human rights abuses, and censorship.[5] The purpose of this law was to force the administration to cut off the funds that maintain the Kim regime and to send an unequivocal message to Chinese, Russian, and other third party banks that either they can do business with North Korea or the U.S. but not both. Congress made those sanctions mandatory precisely to make the Obama administration enforce U.S. law.

But the Obama administration has been slow to sanction any of the dozens of third-country enablers of North Korea proliferation and money laundering even after the report from the U.N. Panel of Experts came out which catalogued a long of list of third party enablers, such as China-based trading companies, banks, and middle-men. In a rare proliferation financing prosecution, the Singapore District Court charged Chinpo Shipping Company and its director for financing North Korean weapons smuggling and proliferation (Chinpo's outward remittances on behalf of North Korea

---

[2]Matthew Carney, "Inside the Chinese border town sustaining North Korea's rogue regime," Australian Broadcasting Corporation, September 11, 2016. http://mobile.abc.net.au/news/2016-09-11/chinese-north-korean-trade-at-dandong-ignores-sanctions/7832178

[3]"Trade in North Korean gold, coal and iron to China continues in April," NK Pro, June 17, 2016. https://www.nknews.org/pro/trade-in-north-korean-gold-coal-and-iron-to-china-continues-in-april/

[4]Anna Fifield, "U.S. Policy on North Korea Relies on China—and Provokes It at the Same Time," *The Washington Post*, August 23, 2016.

[5] North Korea Sanctions and Policy Enforcement Act of 2016. https://www.congress.gov/bill/114th-congress/house-bill/757/text/enr?q=%7B%22search%22%3A%5B%22%5C%22hr757%5C%22%22%5D%7D&resultIndex=1

nationals totaled $40 million).[6] But so far no action has been taken against the Singapore branch of Bank of China, which financed Chipo's transactions and whose staff knowingly deceived their U.S. correspondents by directing Chinpo to conceal any North Korean links to the shipment.[7] As Joshua Stanton notes, whether Bank of China knew the ultimate purpose of the transaction is no defense when its legal obligations were to perform due diligence on its customers, particularly customers linked to North Korea.[8]

Fortunately, when the Congress passed the North Korea Sanctions and Policy Enhancement Act, Congress also included reporting requirements, including a requirement that the administration report to Congress 180 days after the enactment of the legislation on exactly what it has done to enforce the new sanctions. The time has now come for the Congress to hold the administration accountable on what it has done to enforce U.S. law and ask the administration why it has not imposed any secondary sanctions against third-party North Korea enablers.

Secondary sanctions are essential to making North Korea sanctions work, just as they were essential to making Iran sanctions work. History gives us a useful example on this. In September 2005, the U.S. Treasury Department designated Macau-based Banco Delta Asia for laundering North Korea's counterfeit dollars, which led to the blocking of $25 million in North Korean deposits. This action blocked one of the key streams of hard currency for sustaining the Kim regime. A North Korean officer told a U.S. official that the U.S. has finally found a way to hurt the Kim regime. The North eventually returned to the talks and agreed to give up its nuclear weapons program after the U.S. agreed to return the funds to the Kim regime. Unfortunately, after this important leverage has been traded away, the talks fell apart over verification of the North's disarmament. What the case showed is that third countries, in this case, China, will comply with sanctions if its banks face real consequences for conducting illicit business with North Korea. As the Iran nuclear deal ultimately showed, sanctions can get results but only if they are tough, implemented, and sustained over several years. This requires political will on the part of the U.S. government, particularly a willingness to sanction third-country entities that facilitate North Korea's illicit activities and proliferation.

In addition to enforcing the existing sanctions, the next steps are to close loopholes and add even more individuals and entities to the list to further confront North Korea with a clear choice between keeping its nuclear program and regime survival. For example, the administration should work to close the "livelihood" loophole in the coal and iron export sanctions of UNSCR 2270. As it stands, the UN resolution prohibits North Korea from selling coal, iron, or iron ore unless the

---

[6] See UN Security Council, Report of Panel of Experts, February 24, 2016, Section E, "Chinpo Shipping and Financing of Proliferation," 65.
http://www.un.org/ga/search/view_doc.asp?symbol=s/2016/157
[7] Ibid.
[8] See Joshua Stanton's One Free Korea blog. http://freekorea.us/2016/03/09/u-n-report-bank-of-china-helped-shipper-to-hide-n-korean-connections-for-illegal-arms-deal/

transactions "are determined to be exclusively for livelihood purposes." The sanctions would be much tighter and easier to enforce without this loophole.

We can also ban North Korea's exports of food and labor they rely on for hard currency and add more entities to the sanctions list. The North Korean regime sends more than 50,000 people to work abroad in conditions that amount to forced labor to circumvent UN sanctions and earn hard currency for the regime. The vast majority of them are working in China and Russia in mining, logging, textile and construction, but they are also in Africa, Europe, the Middle East and Southeast Asia.[9] Marzuki Darusman, the special rapporteur on human rights in North Korea, stated in a report to the UN Assembly a year ago that these workers are providing up to $2 billion annually.[10] The U.S. needs to call out and pressure the various host countries to stop accepting these North Korean workers.

There are also other entities that could be added to the list. Chairman Royce pointed out, for example, that we can add to the list the state-owned Koryo airline, which continues to "flagrantly violate the ban on luxury goods and [is] implicated in the proliferation of Scud missile parts."[11] In addition, Chairman Royce is also correct to point out that the administration should work with European governments to better block luxury items—including cars, watches, and liquor—from reaching the North Korean ruling elite.[12] Thus far, the Kim regime has managed to keep the flow of luxury goods to the elite class. Cutting off this flow should be an even greater priority for us.

We should also work to disconnect North Korean banks from the Society for Worldwide Interbank Financial Telecommunications (SWIFT) system. Security firm Symantec has linked the hackers who stole $81 million from a bank in Bangladesh in early February to North Korea. Symantec researchers say that they have found evidence that the same hackers hit a bank in the Philippines and attempted to steal over $1 million from a bank in Vietnam. One of the pieces of malware used in the targeted attacks on these Southeast Asian banks has been used by Lazarus, a hacking group that has been linked to North Korea and also targeted U.S. and South Korean assets. The hackers reportedly deployed a rare piece of code that had been seen in only two cases in the past—the hacking attack at Sony Pictures in December 2014 and attacks on South Korea's banks and media companies in 2013, both of which were conducted by North Korea. In Iran's case, even though it was controversial, Congress introduced legislation that would authorize sanctions against SWIFT and the EU passed sanctions regulations of its own on Iranian banks. SWIFT in the end cut off 30 Iranian banks, including its Central Bank. Similar effort

---

[9]"UN investigator: North Koreans doing forced labor abroad to earn foreign currency for country," *Associated Press*, October 28.

[10]Ibid.

[11]"Chairman Royce Condemns Apparent North Korean Nuclear Test," US House Committee on Foreign Affairs, September 9, 2016. http://foreignaffairs.co.nz/2016/09/09/chairman-royce-condemns-apparent-north-korean-nuclear-test/

[12] Ibid.

should be now undertaken against North Korea to remove North Korea from SWIFT and other financial messaging services.

Beyond Sanctions: Containment, Subversion, Diplomacy and Deterrence

In addition to these sanctions measures, there are other actions the administration should pursue to ratchet up pressure on the regime. This requires a multipronged strategy. It includes strengthening deterrence by enhancing missile defense systems around the Korean peninsula, including deployment of the terminal high altitude air defense missile (THAAD) system to South Korea. The Park Geun-hye government has so far stood up to Chinese pressure and domestic opposition in her decision to deploy THAAD. Deployment should be sped up so it doesn't wait until next year. Next steps should include integrating South Korea into the comprehensive U.S.-run ballistic missile defense network and deploying more advanced air and naval assets, including sea-based ballistic missile defenses, against the North Korean submarine missile threat.

We should actively look into ways to increase both funding and means of information dissemination in to North Korea and come up with a comprehensive strategy to help the people of North Korea break the information blockade imposed by the state. Historically, the North Korean regime has been able to maintain tight control over the population by indoctrination and maintaining a monopoly on information. But unofficial information is already increasingly seeping into the North over the porous border with China, chipping away at regime myths and undermining the solidarity of the North Korean people. One South Korean academic who visited a region in China on the border with North Korea a few years ago noted that an MP5 mobile player, which costs about $20 then, is being sold widely in the North, boosting the spread of South Korean dramas and film.[13] We should look into ways to increase our efforts to support radio broadcasts and other means—including covert action—to transmit targeted information into North Korea.

North Korea should be also placed back on the State Sponsors of Terrorism list. Despite the State Department's reluctance to put it back since North Korea was removed in 2008, I believe we can find a legal justification to do so. There is mounting evidence that the Kim regime provided support to terrorist groups, shipping arms to Hamas and Hezbollah. One can also cite a long record of regime attempts to assassinate human rights activists and North Korean defectors, its assistance of Syria's chemical weapons program, not to mention extensive cyber-attacks conducted against South Korea and the U.S. in recent years, including the Sony hacking incident.

---

[13] "Analysts say Hallyu is Moving Fast in the North," *Korea Joongang Daily*, July 31, 2014.

Finally, as we continue with our various attempts to ratchet up pressure on the North, we need to continue to strengthen effective our alliance with South Korea and Japan. We also need to continue our efforts to pressure/lobby China and hold discussions with Beijing not only on North Korea's nuclear program but on potential contingencies in North Korea, including instability scenarios and the possibility of unification. While Beijing's core strategy toward North Korea has not changed and is unlikely to change anytime soon, the strains between Beijing and Pyongyang and Beijing's worries over the increasing possibility of instability in the North suggest there is an opportunity to launch more serious talks with China to take advantage of its concerns. Instead of standing by, hoping that China will change its policy toward the North on its own, the U.S. should be working hard in behind-the-scenes talks to make China understand that a unified Korea—or at the very least a North Korea with a new, reformist regime on the Chinese model—could be in its interest as well as ours, and that continuing to provide the Kim family dynasty with a virtual blank check is a strategic liability for China.

Reaching such an understanding with Beijing is, to be sure, a long shot, but I believe it is more feasible now than in the past. As controversial as this may be, the U.S. could assuage China's main security concerns by pledging not to deploy our troops north of the 38th parallel even if Korea were unified. We could even pledge to withdraw our troops altogether from the peninsula in the event of unification if that's what it takes to win Chinese support for such a path forward. At the end, the odds of a breakthrough with Beijing are slim, but the initiation of such talks, and their continuation over an extended period, is nonetheless useful as it could increase China's comfort level with regime change in North Korea and could eventually pave the way for Beijing to scale back or even end its subsidies to Pyongyang.

Conclusions: Promoting Unification

Even as we push for enforcement of sanctions and ratcheting up pressure on the Kim regime, I am fully aware that these measures too could ultimately fail in bringing about change in the North. The Kim regime may very well never give up its nuclear weapons program and its brinkmanship tactics, and no amount of pressure is guaranteed to change the regime's calculus. Nonetheless, after more than two decades of dealing with North Korea, we are left with few options. We've already tried diplomacy and various negotiations with the North for several decades. Since the October 12, 1994, Agreed Framework, there have been many talks and even agreements, but all agreements eventually broke down as the North could not accept the verification requirements needed to insure that it was keeping its part of the bargain. If we manage to enforce sanctions, including secondary sanctions over a sustained period of time, this would for the first time decisively raise the cost for North Korea of its pursuit of a nuclear weapons program, and this might make Pyongyang reconsider its policies.

Let's assume, however, that the critics of sanctions policy are right and that even the strictest enforcement of sanctions will not make North Korea reconsider its nuclear program. Even so, enforcement of sanctions and a containment policy is still useful. First, North Korea can be an object case to send a message to other rogue regimes around the world that there will be significant cost for flouting international law. Second, sanctions and containment could weaken Kim Jong-un's grip on power and might precipitate regime instability—an outcome we should ultimately welcome, not fear, because we should be pursuing a policy of Korean unification.

Whatever North Korea's immediate future, there is no question that over the long-term its prospects are bleak. While Kim Jong-un's hold on power seems strong for now, there is a sign of growing discord among the ruling class as it struggles for power and influence. We have recently seen increasing rate of defection by fairly high-ranking elites, including a North Korean general and diplomats such as the Deputy Ambassador to the United Kingdom, Thae Yong-ho. A key reason why the North Korean state has been able to persist for this long has been the Kims' ability to maintain the support of powerbrokers in the party, the military, and the government. Frequent purges and executions of high-level elites in recent years may help to strengthen Kim's rule in the short-run by terrorizing potential rivals within the regime. But fundamentally his heavy-handed rule is more likely to corrode long-term elite support of the regime as these purges and executions raise questions in the minds of North Korean elites of their physical safety and whether the 31-year-old heir to the throne is worthy of their trust. The elites must know that if Kim can turn on his uncle and other very senior elites, any of them could be next in his gun-sights.

This is where sanctions enforcement will help. The more we intensify economic pressure against the regime, the more we shake the confidence of the elites and threaten to stir discontent among the people that Kim relies on for support. The more we enforce sanctions, the more Kim Jong-un will be left vulnerable as he will have less foreign currency to underwrite the lifestyles of the North Korean elite whose support is essential to maintaining his grip on power. At the end of the day, it the North's policy will likely change only if a fundamentally different leadership emerges. Tightening the sanctions screws can help hasten that day even if it doesn't lead to an immediate termination of North Korea's nuclear program.

Mr. SALMON. Thank you.
Mr. Albright.

STATEMENT OF MR. DAVID ALBRIGHT, PRESIDENT AND FOUNDER, INSTITUTE FOR SCIENCE AND INTERNATIONAL SECURITY

Mr. ALBRIGHT. Thank you, Mr. Chairman, Ranking Member Sherman, and distinguished members of the subcommittee, for holding this hearing.

North Korea's recent nuclear test, its second this year, demonstrates its resolve and commitment to developing a nuclear arsenal able to strike its enemies. Reversing that growing threat must be a greater U.S. priority. This test, its largest to date, combined with a number of recent ballistic missile tests, should lead the United States and its partners to accept that North Korea can strike its neighbors with nuclear weapons, and it is making progress on building a long-range nuclear-capable force.

Diplomatic efforts so far have proven inadequate to stop North Korea's progress. However, when agreements were reached, they improved transparency over North Korea's nuclear programs, slowed its progress, and led to fewer regional provocations by the regime. In short, negotiating with North Korea is a strategy that can yield both short- and long-term gains. The United States needs to reinvigorate its efforts to seek the dismantlement of North Korea's nuclear arsenal for sure.

With regards to that endeavor, it has to be recognized that China is not going to deliver North Korea's denuclearization. Unless China dramatically changes its current policies, it is not going to institute sanctions or other measures that it views as risking the collapse of the North Korean regime. Although we at my institute support increasing pressure on China to apply more effective sanctions on North Korea, the United States cannot rely on China to press hard enough to get North Korea to make significant nuclear concessions. The United States needs to find additional ways to influence North Korea, including direct negotiations.

At my institute, we are still assessing the recent test, but based on North Korea's statements and the yield of the test, we preliminarily assessed that North Korea may have a family of relatively reliable miniaturized fission weapons with a destructive force rivaling the size of the Hiroshima blast that can use plutonium or weapons-grade uranium and fit on a number of ballistic missiles. North Korea's statement after the test implies that North Korea could have learned to use weapons-grade uranium in what it has called the standardization of the nuclear warhead. This opens the path to building a large number of miniaturized nuclear weapons using weapons-grade uranium. North Korea is likely to be able to produce considerably more weapons-grade uranium than plutonium and in ways that largely escape our current detection.

Taking account of the recent tests, my institute estimates that North Korea has about 12 to over 20 nuclear weapons. We believe, over the next 5 to 10 years, it can significantly increase the number of weapons.

There remains plenty of room to improve and strengthen the sanctions on North Korea. To my institute, the immediate priority is the United States sanctioning Chinese companies involved in providing controlled or sensitive goods to North Korea. The U.S. Government should use its authority to sanction illicit actors in China that supply North Korea's nuclear missile and other nuclear programs. In addition, in order to prevent the further expansion of North Korea's nuclear programs, more coordination is needed among allies to thwart North Korea's overseas purchases for its nuclear and missile programs. It is also useful to step up sanctioning of banks and financial institutions involved in business with North Korean nuclear missile and military programs.

Reestablishing meaningful negotiations with North Korea will not be easy, but it should be a major U.S. priority. How to achieve meaningful denuclearization negotiations, and what they should cover requires much deeper study, but any negotiation should be premised on a firm commitment to achieve North Korean denuclearization and avoid in any way legitimizing North Korean nuclear weapons. These negotiations should include broader initial declarations of its uranium and plutonium pathways to the bomb and provide access to nuclear sites outside of the Yongbyon complex.

Moreover, the negotiations cannot focus only on the nuclear program. They will need to ratchet back North Korea's ballistic missile programs and resolve regional security issues. Finally, North Korea must commit to not proliferate abroad and not to engage in nuclear and missile cooperation with Iran or other countries.

Congress has an important role in establishing U.S. sanctions and sanctions policy on North Korea, and it should encourage the administration to use its authorities given in the North Korea Sanctions and Policy Enhancement Act of 2016. It should also explore more ways to encourage China to apply sanctions on North Korea. However, as I have said, the United States should not depend solely on China. It also needs to develop other ways to influence North Korea to denuclearize. Engaging North Korea has historically shown that it yields limitations and more transparency into North Korea's nuclear activities compared to a policy of ignoring the threat while it grows. Combined with greater efforts to rein in its illicit activities and addressing regional security concerns, changing the status quo of North Korea's ongoing dangerous provocations is possible. New thinking is needed to reengage this dangerous regime and start the process of achieving denuclearization. Thank you.

[The prepared statement of Mr. Albright follows:]

Testimony of David Albright,
President of the
Institute for Science and International Security,
before the House Foreign Affairs
Subcommittee on Asia and the Pacific

Hearing Title: "North Korea's Perpetual Provocations:
Another Dangerous, Escalatory Nuclear Test"

September 14, 2016

North Korea's September 9, 2016 nuclear test, its second this year, demonstrates its resolve and commitment to developing a nuclear arsenal able to strike its enemies. Reversing that growing threat must be a greater United States priority.

This test, its largest to date, combined with a number of recent ballistic missile tests, should also lead the United States and its partners to accept that North Korea can strike its neighbors with nuclear weapons and is making progress on building a long-range nuclear-capable force. Although we share the assessment that North Korea will likely need several more years before it can deploy a nuclear-tipped intercontinental ballistic missile (ICBM) that can strike the United States, North Korea appears embarked on a path to succeed in that endeavor.

Diplomatic efforts so far have proven inadequate to stop North Korea's progress. However, when agreements were reached, they improved transparency over North Korea's nuclear programs, slowed its progress, and led to fewer regional provocations by the regime. In short, negotiating with North Korea is a strategy that can yield both short and long term gains. The United States needs to reinvigorate its efforts to seek the dismantlement of North Korea's nuclear arsenal. With regards to that endeavor, it has to be recognized that China is not going to deliver North Korea's denuclearization. Unless China dramatically changes its current policies, it is not going to institute sanctions or other measures that it views as risking the collapse of the North Korean regime. Although we support increasing pressure on China to apply more effective sanctions on North Korea, the United States cannot rely on China to press hard enough to get North Korea to make significant nuclear concessions. The United States needs to find additional ways to influence North Korea, including direct negotiations.

North Korea does face limitations and hardships in further mastering nuclear weapons and building more advanced ones. There is room for counterproliferation efforts to learn about and inhibit its nuclear weapons program and for international efforts to disrupt its progress. As demonstrated by its growing capabilities, there is a dire need to reevaluate and reenergize current policies aimed at denuclearizing the Korean Peninsula. If US policy does not become more effective, North Korea will likely succeed in eventually creating a much larger, deadlier nuclear force – my Institute estimates up to 50-100 nuclear weapons in the next five years – and perhaps proliferate its capabilities to other nations, while increasing its provocations regionally. This is a threat that the United States must do more to head off.

Recent Test

The September 9 nuclear test had the largest seismic signal of any of North Korea's five confirmed tests. My Institute preliminarily estimates the explosive yield as 10-15 kilotons, where the upper value is about the same as the Hiroshima blast. However, beyond the seismic signal, scientific data about the test at least publicly remain unavailable. Questions include: was the test one that used only plutonium or weapon-grade uranium, or both? Was there any thermonuclear material involved that increased the yield of the test?

A North Korean statement issued soon after the test, which should be greeted with skepticism absent other information, allows our preliminary interpretation. Our interpretation can be summarized as follows:

> North Korea appears to have a family of relatively reliable, miniaturized fission weapons with the destructive force rivalling the size of the Hiroshima blast that can use plutonium or weapon-grade uranium and fit on a number of ballistic missiles.

More data are needed to confirm the various parts of our interpretation but we see no evidence contradicting this assessment. The statement implies that North Korea could have learned to use weapon-grade uranium in what it has called the "standardization of the nuclear warhead." This opens the path to building a large number of miniaturized nuclear weapons using weapon-grade uranium. North Korea is likely to be able to produce considerably more weapon-grade uranium than plutonium.

It should be noted that the recent North Korean statement is very different in nature than the one following its January 2016 test, where it proclaimed it had detonated a thermonuclear weapon. The seismic evidence supports that the explosive yield was not in line with a thermonuclear weapon. But even in the absence of a successful thermonuclear test, one should take note of the direction of North Korea's nuclear weapons effort and it is reasonable to skeptically accept that North Korea is working on some type of thermonuclear device, likely one aimed at using thermonuclear materials to significantly boost the yield of a fission device. Earlier, in a worst-case assessment, we projected that North Korea could field a crude thermonuclear weapon with a yield approaching 100 kilotons soon after 2020. If North Korea continues its aggressive nuclear testing program, it could achieve that goal sooner.

Estimated Number of Nuclear Weapons

North Korea has an extensive nuclear program aimed at producing nuclear explosive materials for making nuclear weapons. Many of its nuclear facilities, e.g. those at Yongbyon, are known. However, a great deal of its nuclear capability is unknown or just suspected. Its nuclear capability has also depended on wide ranging overseas illicit procurements.

North Korea has developed successfully both the means to produce plutonium and weapon-grade uranium. Its stock of plutonium appears limited, but it appears to have a substantial capacity to produce weapon-grade uranium at both known and suspected locations.

As of June 2016, before the latest test, my Institute estimated that North Korea had about 13-21 nuclear weapons made from either plutonium or weapon-grade uranium. In this estimate, we ignored the potential production of weapon-grade uranium at a second, unknown enrichment plant, which using our methodology would increase the upper bound of nuclear weapons above 21 but not increase the lower bound. (The lower bound assumes that a second plant does not exist or contributes minimally to the total quantity of WGU, such as if the plant only took low enriched uranium produced at the Yongbyon enrichment plant and further enriched it to weapon-grade uranium).

Taking account of the recent test, the estimate becomes a total of 12-20 nuclear weapons. This estimate, despite not being comprehensive, suggests that North Korea is able to produce a sizeable number of nuclear weapons.

The estimate of North Korea's arsenal depends on an assumption that North Korea makes nuclear weapons using weapon-grade uranium. Its plutonium supply is limited. As such, this estimate remains uncertain, since so little is known about its enrichment activities or use of weapon-grade uranium in nuclear weapons. However, as mentioned above, another reason to be concerned about this recent test is that North Korea's statement implies that its nuclear weapons are no longer just plutonium based. But overall, more information about North Korea's ability to make plutonium, weapon-grade uranium, and nuclear weapons is needed.

Over the next five years, we have projected that under a certain set of conditions, that North Korea could achieve a nuclear arsenal of up to 50-100 nuclear weapons. Its pace of nuclear testing supports such a projection.

Foreign Procurements for its Nuclear Programs

North Korea has depended on illegal or questionable procurements for decades for its nuclear and other military programs, in particular seeking European, Japanese, and US goods. When it could no longer base its operations in Europe in the early 2000s, it shifted its operations to China where such operations have been centered since then. Operating in China, it has acquired a wide range of goods from Chinese companies and middlemen, as well as from US, Japanese, and European subsidiaries, which have been deceived into thinking they were selling to Chinese end users. China has not done an adequate job of enforcing its export control and sanctions laws against these illegal exports and retransfers to North Korea.

A new United Nations Security Council (UNSC) sanctions resolution, Resolution 2270, passed in March 2016, has put additional pressure on China to stem this flow of goods to North Korea. It is too early to judge the effects of the new sanctions on inhibiting North Korea's efforts to outfit its nuclear programs. However, preliminary information suggests that China is still not doing enough.

There remains plenty of room to improve and strengthen the sanctions on North Korea. The idea that they have failed or somehow improved North Korea's illicit procurement capabilities is false; more accurately, the sanctions have simply not been implemented strongly enough by China, North Korea's main illicit procurement source.

To my Institute, the immediate priority is the United States sanctioning Chinese companies involved in providing controlled or sensitive goods to North Korea. My Institute has the name of at least one company engaged in recent illicit activity that deserves immediate sanctioning. There are likely many others known to the US government that could be sanctioned. The US government should use its authority to sanction illicit actors in China that supply North Korea's nuclear, missile, and other military programs.

In addition, in order to prevent the further expansion of North Korea's nuclear programs, more coordination is needed among allies to thwart North Korea's overseas purchases for its nuclear programs. It is also useful to step up sanctioning of banks and financial institutions involved in business with North Korean nuclear, missile, and military programs.

Negotiations

Reestablishing meaningful negotiations with North Korea will not be easy but it should be a major US priority. Over the last 25 years, there have been several efforts that have successfully delayed North Korea's nuclear progress or come close to making real progress on denuclearization. But they ultimately failed. Generally, these negotiations were premised on North Korea either not having nuclear weapons or having at most a few. That assumption is no longer viable and the negotiating strategy needs to reflect this shift.

There may be a temptation to replace the long-established goal of North Korean denuclearization with the goal of focusing on limiting North Korea's nuclear advances. But dropping or de-emphasizing denuclearization risks legitimizing North Korea's nuclear weapons programs while offering little in the way of preventing further nuclear proliferation or even military conflict in the region. Although achieving denuclearization looks bleak today, it should remain the fundamental driving goal of the United States.

How to achieve negotiations and what they should cover requires much deeper study. The current model of essentially relying on a reluctant China to rein in North Korea has not worked and is unlikely to do so as North Korea grows its nuclear capabilities. Although increasing sanctions and pressure on North Korea makes sense, it no longer seems that such a policy can work outside a broader, targeted US approach aimed at achieving nuclear limitations and reductions.

Establishing intermediate limits on North Korea's nuclear weapons program has to be part of any denuclearization strategy. However, as mentioned above, they should avoid legitimizing in any way North Korea's nuclear weapons, as happened after the 1998 nuclear tests by Pakistan and India.

Although the North Korean nuclear situation is in many ways unique and certainly has a long and tortuous history, we should look for lessons in the cases of South Africa's and Libya's denuclearization rather than the cases of India and Pakistan, or even Iran. Critical to South

Africa's denuclearization was the parallel negotiations on resolving or mitigating regional security issues that inflamed nuclear weapon ambitions. How such discussions could be established in North Asia needs a fresh look.

Another lesson of South Africa is that a nuclear warhead cannot be meaningfully isolated from its delivery systems, such as ballistic missiles. Both are needed for a nuclear arsenal. Any negotiations involving North Korea must include its ballistic missiles.

Establishing international verification in North Korea, even initially, will need to include declarations about North Korea's uranium pathway to the bomb. Too much of North Korea's capability to make nuclear explosive materials and nuclear weapons remains hidden. Any negotiations should emphasize early the need for a broader North Korean declaration of its nuclear infrastructure, including previously undeclared nuclear facilities and nuclear weapons.

The old models of focusing on freezing or disabling and then monitoring nuclear activity only at the Yongbyon site are no longer practical. New arrangements will need more robust inspections than the traditional, weak monitoring associated with past agreements and have access to sites outside Yongbyon.

As the United States strives for negotiations, allied governments need to cooperate more in order to determine North Korea's undeclared nuclear infrastructure and estimate with more certainty the size of its nuclear arsenal. Much more of this work should be made public.

Any negotiations need to obtain North Korean assurances early in the process that it is not spreading dangerous weapons, materials, and technologies abroad and is not engaging in nuclear and missile cooperation with Iran.

Conclusion

Congress has an important role in establishing US sanctions and sanctions policy on North Korea. It should encourage the administration to use its authorities given in the North Korean Sanctions and Policy Enhancement Act of 2016. It should also explore more ways to encourage China to apply sanctions on North Korea.

However, the United States should not depend solely on China. It also needs to develop other ways to influence North Korea to denuclearize.

Engaging North Korea has historically shown that it yields limitations and more transparency into North Korea's nuclear activities compared to a policy of ignoring the threat while it grows. Combined with greater efforts to reign in its illicit activities and addressing regional security concerns, changing the status quo of North Korea's ongoing dangerous provocations is possible. New thinking is needed to re-engage this dangerous regime and make steps toward the goal of denuclearization.

What should one make of the January 6, 2016 test and North Korea's claims about thermonuclear weapons?

North Korea announced after its January 2016 test that it had detonated a thermonuclear weapon but this announcement was greeted with great disbelief. Seismic data did not reveal a large explosion; a larger yield would be expected for a thermonuclear or boosted device. However, the test was detonated at about double the depth of the test in 2013. This could imply that North Korea expected a larger yield and the design failed.

So far, there is no data from radioactive releases that could shed light on the nature of the January test. Nonetheless, it is reasonable to skeptically accept that North Korea is working on some type of thermonuclear device.

Indirect evidence for work on thermonuclear weapons includes:

- North Korea has constructed a plant to make lithium 6, a key material to produce thermonuclear weapons.
- North Korea is also assessed as pursuing tritium production and separation.
- It has expressed interest in statements and via procurements of tritium capabilities.
- The 5 megawatt-thermal (MWth) reactor has channels for isotope production, including tritium production in lithium 6 targets
- Its IRT reactor may be operational again, which can make small quantities of tritium.
- North Korea has a capability to separate tritium in the Isotope Production Laboratory near the IRT reactor.
- It may be building an isotope separation plant at Yongbyon able to separate tritium from lithium-6 targets.

Realistically, North Korea is unlikely to be close to testing an H bomb, which is generally considered to be a two-stage fission-fusion-fission device. Such a device is highly sophisticated and capable of achieving 1000s of kilotons of explosive yield. The US type of boosted fission device with a tritium/deuterium gas injected into the center of the device also appears beyond the reach of North Korea today.

What seems more within North Korea's capabilities includes the type of device South Africa explored in its nuclear weapons program, namely a device with a lithium-deuterium-tritium tablet at the center of an atomic device with a goal to achieve a device with 60-100 kilotons. North Korea could also be seeking to use a more sophisticated version of that idea by considering shells of thermonuclear material placed around a fission design. A more sophisticated example, and one possibly achievable by North Korea if it continues nuclear testing, is a one stage thermonuclear device. This design would use a plutonium core with thermonuclear material in shells around the plutonium core and also with shells of weapon-grade uranium. A British one-stage thermonuclear device tested in mid-1950s with a plutonium core, thermonuclear material, and 100 kg of weapon-grade uranium in shells achieved an explosive yield of several hundred kilotons.

Mr. SALMON. Thank you. I appreciate the witnesses' comments.

The United States has engaged in negotiations with North Korea in the past from time to time during the Bush administration. We agreed to certain lifting of sanctions at the commitment that Korea would do certain things. We lifted the sanctions, started the flow back into North Korea, and quickly found out that it was a ruse. They went back to doing exactly what they did before.

While, Mr. Albright, I don't discount the importance of diplomacy and negotiations, I don't think most of us are very trustful that Kim Jong-un is an honest broker and that he is somebody that we can count on to keep his word once he gives it. I think that the sanctions that we have employed heretofore, both by the United States and the international community at large, have been largely unsuccessful in getting any kind of change or desired change from North Korea. And, I am increasingly believing that China's intransigence on the issue is becoming more and more frustrating. On one hand, they loudly proclaim that they are just as committed to stopping the proliferation of nuclear weapons in North Korea as the rest of us are, but yet they are really not doing that which they can to make change.

The chief reason is, as I have talked with some of our Chinese diplomats, they say it is their concern that there will be a flood of refugees over the China border if they impose the kind of sanctions, economic and otherwise, that would really motivate North Korea that it could implode their economy. So, there is a fear of that.

I am not sure that I buy that. In fact, I kind of almost feel like, on one side, they are saying, ''Don't do it''; on the other side, you know, they are allowing many of their companies to provide the wherewithal to increase that nuclear program.

I would really like to explore more ideas. I mean, we have talked about the deployment of THAAD on the Korean Peninsula, which I strongly support. In fact, we just passed a bill that I and Brad Sherman authored dealing with trilateral relationship between us, Japan, and South Korea, but also strong language in there about the deployment of THAAD on the Korean Peninsula. So, on one hand, that, you know, is a step in the right direction, but China is also using all their political influences to pressure China—or, excuse me, pressure Seoul not to do that. In fact, that is probably one of the biggest sources of political blowback that they are getting to getting it done, because South Korea counts on China very heavily in their economic projections and economic strength. So that kind of pressure from China is very inordinate.

What are some of the other things that we can do to get China to the table? I agree with targeted sanctions against Chinese companies that are in the mix, you know, with this Chinese—or excuse me, this North Korean proliferation. But Mr. Sherman has suggested at times past—I think it is kind of provocative—maybe we should be looking at other potential economic sanctions against China because of their lack of interest in getting this done. And I am asking, you know, what are your thoughts on that? Are those possible motivators?

The other thing that I am wondering is—I know when it was said during the campaign, a lot of people got real excited, but what is the likelihood that China and South Korea at some point in time, if North Korea develops a really robust nuclear program and it is proven to be reliable, what is the likelihood that South Korea and Japan, those two entities, might start looking at their own nuclear programs in a defensive realm? Those are my thoughts.

And, Dr. Cha, would you maybe start off your response?

Mr. CHA. Thank you, Chairman. I will try to address a couple of these. I think they are all very important points, and I think you have framed the policy problem quite well.

Let me just say, on negotiations, as someone who participated in the last set of negotiations, the 2005-2007 Six Party Agreed Framework, I know what that rabbit hole looks like. And it will start out with—in terms of what we could get. It will start out with a ban on—they will self-declare a testing ban as long as we are in talks with them. And then, if we are lucky, we might get a freeze on operations at the 5-megawatt reactor at Yongbyon. I think that will be about as far as we can get during the course of negotiations.

That freeze won't be verifiable in the sense that they won't let the IAEA in, I don't think. And, of course, it won't include anything outside of Yongbyon, even the one facility that they have said is a uranium facility at Yongbyon. So I think it is going to be—so we have been down that rabbit hole. And it will do something, but, at best, it is a holding position and a suboptimal holding position. So I am also one for negotiations, but it is going to be very difficult.

On what we should do, I mean, I think there are two areas of vulnerability that we should press on. With regard to China, China doesn't respond to what North Korea does. China responds to what the United States does in response to North Korea. And whether it is secondary sanctioning or even something that is a little bit more radical, including possibly altering the disposition of our forces on the peninsula in a way that makes our overall capabilities more robust but makes our forces less vulnerable. That would be something China would take notice of.

And, with regard to North Korea, you have already hit on it. Both of you have hit on it, and that is the information issue. That is what they see as a vulnerability. But, the thing is, either of these things entails more risk on the part of the United States and our policies on this issue. What we see thus far, what we all find so distasteful, the current position, is because we have generally been quite risk-averse when it comes to dealing with this problem. But, it has grown so out of control that some of these other measures we might consider that press on vulnerabilities of both China and North Korea are there, but it requires us being willing to take on more risk.

Mr. SALMON. I am going to yield to the next question, but the risk of the status quo is far worse than anything that you are talking about as far as what those risks entail, I believe. The risk of just allowing it to go as it is going right now is a very frightening venture, and I think that if we are doing risk assessment, you got to take that into account as well.

Mr. Lowenthal.

Mr. LOWENTHAL. Thank you, Mr. Chair.

I would like to follow up on your questioning now. After listening, I find this fascinating.

I have heard a lot about, you know, China and China's intransigence and lack of compliance to really helping, especially in terms of—and then the response of, what kinds of pressure can we put on?

What about other kinds of alternatives? I am not really understanding very well the role of China in the sense that, is there a way that we can enlist China as a partner, not as an adversary in this relationship, but as a partner in terms of what does China fear about North Korea's weakness? Does China need North Korea strong, or would they like to see something different, and what are they frightened of? And what does China want in all of this? I am not hearing, what would China want in something like this? Because I am just hearing one side, what we want, what we do. And I agree with that. But what does China want in this relationship, and are they frightened of something? I would like to kind of understand more if we are really talking about other kinds of alternatives. Anybody?

Ms. TERRY. Yes. I would like to just discuss some of the points that the chairman and you have just made. And China, just briefly to go over your point, I think economic sanctions, trade, it is all good, but there is no political will in the Obama administration. So I think we really need to still focus on the secondary sanctions and target Bank of China, Bank of Daedong, Chinpo Shipping, and so on.

Regarding your point about what does China fear, I think part of what we can discuss with China is that China fears instability in the Korean Peninsula. China fears unification ultimately, because it does not want a pro-U.S. unified Korea with potential U.S. forces on the——

Mr. LOWENTHAL. Is that an obstacle, or could that be a potential for us to have discussions with them?

Ms. TERRY. This is somewhat controversial, but I would like to argue that—in terms of trying to help come up with creative thinking is, say, if you can engage and try to have a candid discussion with China. It would be very difficult to do so, but—not only about the nuclear program, but the potential instability and potential unification scenarios. And, we might have to make that kind of grand bargain where we do sort of promise to reduce U.S. troop presence or even it has to be, post-unification, pulling U.S. forces out. But, that is something that we could consider in addition to just sort of trying to pressure China.

I just want to get back to your point about South Korea and Japan arms race. I think that is a very big concern, that if we let nuclear North Korea happen, ultimately, I think there will be an instability in the region. Because South Korea is already talking about bringing tactical nuclear—some South Koreans are—bringing tactical nuclears back to South Korea, and they will cause arms race both by South Korea and Japan.

Mr. KLINGNER. I would just add, Mr. Albright pointed out the exponentially growing North Korean threat. We have had what to some were sudden unexpected revelations that "gambling was going on in the casino," in that missiles that had been under development for years had success, and that shocked people. So now you

49

have this new fear that the threat is real. It would be humorous if it weren't disturbing.

So we have a submarine-launched ballistic missile which had a breakthrough. The intermediate-range missile had a breakthrough. Guam is now under direct threat. So it is a question of, are we serious or not? There are things we can do at the U.N. We should push for eliminating what is called the "livelihood purposes" loophole on the ban on North Korea's export of resources. The loophole is bigger than the ban.

With regard to China, I think they don't want a crisis on their border, but their behavior is only creating the conditions that will bring about that crisis. The Obama administration and the Bush administration have had conversations with China, trying to explain that their reluctance to pressure their ally is only bringing about the crisis they don't want, and it is only going to cause the U.S. and its allies to take responsive measures that they won't like.

So we can try to induce their cooperation, but when we talk about secondary sanctions on China, we can almost sort of toss that off, but it is actually very, very important, because what it can do is actually induce Chinese banks and businesses to do things that the government doesn't want them to do.

We saw that back in the mid-2000s with Banco Delta Asia. The Chinese Government didn't want Bank of China to cut off North Korea. The Bank of China knew it could be susceptible under U.S. law to being precluded from access to the U.S. financial system. So the Bank of China, in essence, told the government: Well, we hear you, but we have to disagree. We have to cut off North Korea. Otherwise, the Bank of China could face sanctions. So if we were to sanction even one Chinese entity, it would send a very strong signal to the others.

Mr. ALBRIGHT. Could I add to that? Is there still time? Because I think it is very important that the enforcement of the existing sanctions be done rather than—I mean, it is important to look for new ones. I mean, maybe there is a silver bullet out there and maybe SWIFT is potentially that.

But at the same time, it is critical to send a message to China, because another issue with China is that on a lot of these exports to North Korea, it claims it is just a big large developing country that can't manage its own system. And, I think, there is some truth to that. There are hundreds of thousands of companies licensed for export in China. And even if you take a European country, some of the smaller ones, you are talking about hundreds or 1,000 companies that can do that. So the control issues are profound.

But I think that that also creates an opportunity, that China doesn't support these exports, but it is not going to do anything. And I think the U.S. can play a very important role in sending a signal into China that it needs to do it. And I think it is critically important at this time to enforce the sanctions that this Congress has passed. And there are companies in China that are known to deal with North Korea, and strong cases can be made that they are violating the sanctions and the U.S. should actually sanction them.

Mr. SALMON. Thank you.

General Perry.

Mr. SHERMAN. I would ask for 1 minute.

I want to address this issue what I think China would want. I mean, they would prefer if North Korea didn't have a nuclear program, but that is not high on their list. They would like to continue trade. That is not the highest thing on their list. The purpose of sanctions is to force the regime to change its policy by creating regime-threatening sanctions, and China does not want this regime threatened.

And the one thing that they don't want——

Mr. LOWENTHAL. Because of——

Mr. SHERMAN. Because they could see, if this regime implodes, two very bad things happen for China: Millions of very poor North Koreans move north as refugees. And then you might see a unification under the South Korean Government. And unless we promise otherwise and unless they can believe the promise, an American military, not on the 37th, 38th parallel, but right up on their border. So, they don't want an American Army on their border. They don't want the implosion of the regime.

Mr. LOWENTHAL. I agree with all those things that you are saying, but could that be the basis of a discussion?

Mr. SHERMAN. It ought to be, but I will yield back.

Mr. SALMON. Thanks. Congressman Perry.

Mr. PERRY. Thank you, Mr. Chairman.

Dr. Cha, you suggested a new posture or profile for the United States military in South Korea. Can you be specific?

Mr. CHA. Well, I think there is more that we can do in terms of missile defense, not just one THAAD battery, but more than one. My colleague Bruce referenced sea-based platforms in terms of missile defense. SM3, I think that is another name. And these sorts of things will both create better defense of the peninsula and get China's attention.

Mr. PERRY. What about land-based force?

Mr. CHA. So that is the next piece.

Mr. PERRY. And other than missile defense, seagoing missile defense, what about seagoing?

Mr. CHA. Seagoing missile defense——

Mr. PERRY. No, other than missile defense. But I am talking about more robust naval posture. Is that——

Mr. CHA. Yes. I think that, both in Japan and in Hawaii and in Guam, and then the land-based forces on the Korean Peninsula. I mean, there is an argument—I am not necessarily advocating this argument, but there is an argument that could be made in the sense that those forces traditionally have been a tripwire for a second conventional ground invasion. That is not going to happen again. And in that sense, the tripwire concept may not be relevant anymore. There are other ways to defend and maintain the strength of the U.S. extended deterrence on the peninsula that don't require a tripwire and that also don't leave forces vulnerable to chem, bio, or a nuclear attack from the north.

Now, you know, this is not the forum in which to get into details on things of that nature. But, all I am saying is that we should be willing to discuss new things, as the chairman said, new ideas, that make sense in terms of our defense against a nuclear North Korea, but also that are things that can create enough concern in the case of China that they might be willing to change their own risk assessment of pressuring North Korea.

Mr. PERRY. What is South Korea's—how would they view or how would they be interested in increasing those postures, ground forces, sea-based——

Mr. CHA. I think there would be a great deal of interest in things that augment the capabilities, both U.S. and combined capabilities. The ground troops would be a very controversial issue for them, just because there is a legacy issue there.

Mr. PERRY. Right.

Mr. CHA. And that would be very controversial.

Mr. PERRY. Okay. And then one final question from a messaging standpoint or information operations, like the Voice of America, et cetera, how robust is our capability now? Is it used to the fullest extent? What can be done to increase that, or should that be increased? And, does it have any effect at all?

Mr. CHA. It definitely has an effect. Defector testimony shows, not—well, 100 percent of defectors, but defector testimony suggests close to 80 or 90 percent of people inside North Korea have had exposure to a foreign radio broadcast.

This is really a question of resources, I think. The more resources that can be put to this, the more you can enhance that capability. I mean, there is a hardware issue there too, in terms of, you know, where can you bounce these things off? So, I guess you could say that the tube is kind of small, but there is still a lot more that can go into that tube that would have an impact.

Mr. PERRY. What would be North Korea's response to increasing the volume on that? No pun intended.

Mr. CHA. I think the regime would be very sensitive to it. And this is a bigger vulnerability I think for them than THAAD, for example.

Mr. PERRY. When you say "very sensitive," I mean, I am sure they don't want any of it. They don't like what there is now, and they are going to like it less if we do more, but what is our risk in doing more?

Mr. CHA. There is a risk.

Mr. PERRY. What is that risk?

Mr. CHA. Well, in the past, when the South Koreans increased information coming across the border, the North Koreans have threatened to take out the speakers. So there is that risk. There is the risk that they could respond in anger and shell an island. There is definitely a risk to it.

But my point is that these sorts of strategies will necessarily entail more risk. Otherwise, we remain stuck in the current cycle that we are in.

Mr. PERRY. Thanks. Mr. Chairman, I yield.

Ms. TERRY. Can I add a quick comment to that? I spent a lot of time debriefing North Korean defectors. I think information dissemination is one of the keys we have that we can use against the North Korean regime. The risk is that they are going to get angry, but so what? I mean, we are looking for ways to work here. Monopoly on information is one of the pillars of the regime's stability. This is how they were able to survive for this long. So I think finding ways to try and disseminate information into the north is critical for us.

And we have got to find ways to open the Internet to the people of North Korea—I know we have been sort of working on that—so they can have access to information, they can communicate freely with their South Korean brethren and so on. I think there are ways to maybe work with Google and Facebook to pilot their global initiative in North Korea. I think we need to increase the range and power of TVs and AM broadcasting to North Korean audiences and so on. We can work on covert ways. We can work with the intelligence community to find covert ways. Whatever we can to get information into North Korea, I think, is one of the things that we can actually pursue.

Mr. PERRY. Dr. Terry, doesn't that all have to be covert? I mean, we can broadcast as much as we want. We can facilitate some way for them to see the Internet. But if you don't have the hardware and if it is punishable by death to be caught viewing these things——

Ms. TERRY. Sure. Even in overt ways. I think overt ways, covert ways. I am just emphasizing the importance of trying to get information into North Korea.

Mr. PERRY. Thank you.

Mr. SALMON. Thank you. Ms. Gabbard.

Ms. GABBARD. Thank you, Mr. Chairman.

We have seen how hard currency sanctions were more successful than other sanctions in the past. Can you comment on whether or not you think those types of sanctions would be as effective or more effective today, and, if so, why or why not?

Mr. KLINGNER. I think it is first important to point out the multiple objectives that sanctions and targeted financial measures have. Some have said people are already impatient: ''Well, it has been 4 months. Sanctions haven't worked. Let's go back to diplomacy,'' which had 20 years of failure.

But even before it changes North Korea's behavior, it is enforcing U.S. Law. It is imposing a penalty or pain on those that violate our law and U.N. resolutions. It constrains or puts in place measures to constrain the inflow of items for their prohibited nuclear missile programs, including money from illicit activities. It puts into place measures to reduce the risk of proliferation. And then, five, the most difficult in conjunction with all your instruments of national power, it is trying to alter their behavior.

So I would say on four of the five, the sanctions have already been successful to some degree. The fifth is the most difficult. But when we have a very small country with very few avenues of access to the outside world—and that is mainly China—it is I think a better target than Iran.

Some would say: ''Well, you can't sanction Iran, because it is so big, it is so connected with the world, it has got oil, et cetera; go after North Korea.''

Well, now that we had pressure on Iran, which brought about the negotiations, now people are saying: ''Well, that worked because it was so big and so well-connected; it won't work with North Korea.''

I would argue the opposite.

Ms. GABBARD. Interesting.

53

Mr. CHA. May I add?

Ms. GABBARD. Dr. Cha.

Mr. CHA. So I would agree with what Bruce said. I think there are two issues when we are talking about these currency sanctions. I don't know, Representative Gabbard, if your question is suggesting this. But one of them is—however it is—is to reduce the North Koreans to having to carry suitcases of cash if they want to do any sort of transaction. So that is one. And that is the proliferation findings.

The other part—and this is the part that I am not sure if your question is—is the freezing of their assets and accounts overseas because that is a different—that is directly linked to the leadership, right. And that could have a very big impact on how this leadership thinks and addresses and behaves. And so, whatever sanctions the committee is working, whatever legislation, I think these are the two objectives. We want to reduce them to having to carry suitcases of cash, and then we also want to be able to target those assets that we think are connected to the leadership wherever they are. So——

Ms. GABBARD. Thank you.

Mr. Albright.

Mr. ALBRIGHT. Yeah. I think one of the problems, though, is that China resists these kinds of sanctions. I mean, their view is, if you close off the financial system to North Korea, and it is concentrated in certain Chinese banks, it will collapse the state. So you immediately run into this problem where they just don't cooperate.

But at the same time, we don't really know what is going to happen. And I think it is, again, an argument why we need to get the administration to enforce the existing sanctions and target some of these banks, target some of these entities, and then let's see what happens.

One thing—I don't know, I don't want to take your time, but I think, on the engagement, I don't think that we have to accept crumby conditions of engagement, shutting down 5-megawatt reactor—I forget the other condition you gave. I mean, we simply say: No, it is not enough.

And even I was engaged in the discussions on the—before the Leap Day Deal, and North Koreans were willing to shut down and stop the centrifuges at the Pyongyang centrifuge plant. Who knows if they would have followed through. But even that is not enough today. We need to have more than that if there is going to be a negotiation. So I think it is up to us to sculpt the engagement, not to accept kind of the pitiful things that North Korea may offer initially.

Ms. GABBARD. I think that is the remaining question. I don't have time for it now, but, you know, people have raised getting back to the negotiating table, setting the conditions to be able to make that possible, but then addressing the chairman's point about the lack of trust in actually being able to execute knowing that there has to be truly enforceable consequences to noncompliance in that situation.

So thank you all for being here.

Mr. SALMON. Thank you.

Mr. Sherman.

Mr. SHERMAN. Well, if we are going to achieve our political objectives for the foreign policy establishment, et cetera, here in this country, we need to do two things: First, don't make compromises, and don't admit how weak our position is. And, second, cling to the idea that we are somehow going to completely disarm North Korea of all nuclear weapons. And then, third, when we fail to achieve our objectives, which has been true this entire century, just shrug it off, and as long as you don't propose any radical change in policy, the foreign policy establishment will say you know what you are talking about. And the fact that we have totally failed to slow down this program doesn't mean that we haven't achieved the political objectives of all telling each other that we know what we are talking about.

If I gather from your testimony, China is loath to accept regime-threatening sanctions on this regime, and this regime is not going to eliminate its nuclear program unless it faces regime-threatening sanctions. The question here is, is this a regime willing to settle for 10 to 15 nuclear weapons and a lot of monitoring? Because we know that they won't give up all of their nuclear weapons unless they face regime change and regime endangerment.

Will they, just to avoid pressure and get along with China, accept a world in which they are a limited nuclear state? I am not saying that we would make this concession, but how would that look from their standpoint?

Mr. Albright.

Mr. ALBRIGHT. I think they would be interested. I mean, I would be scared to make that kind of concession. It could be very damaging in the region, but I take your point. And I would say that——

Mr. SHERMAN. Are you predicting that, I mean, when you close your eyes and think of the world 15 years from now, do you think that North Korea will have a greater or lesser nuclear capacity than they have today?

Mr. ALBRIGHT. Well, I feel that they are going to have a greater, but we have to be guided by denuclearization in order to ensure——

Mr. SHERMAN. It would be nice to cling to denuclearization, but as I think you predict, I think as most of us would predict, if we keep doing what we have been doing, we are going to get a very similar result, but I want to——

Mr. ALBRIGHT. I am just afraid we are going to get that result if we do accept 15 deliverable nuclear weapons.

Mr. SHERMAN. Okay, keep in mind, unless the regime is truly threatened and close to falling, they are not going to give up their 10 to 15 weapons because they feel they need those to defend themselves from us. And keep in mind, when they asked for a non-aggression treaty, the response from Vice President Cheney was no because we contemplate aggression.

So it is not like I would expect them to completely. But I want to go to a much smaller issue, not that it is a small issue, and that is state sponsor of terrorism designation. The first issue is, is this legally justified? One could argue that, you know, long ago, North Korea kidnapped people. They kidnapped people to make movies. They kidnapped people to get advice on Japanese etiquette. They kidnapped people, and some would say, well, that happened a long time ago so you can't call them a state sponsor of terrorism. But they haven't released them. So it is a continuing act of terrorism. They haven't returned their bodies if they died of natural or unnatural causes. So maybe that is a continuing act of terrorism.

But I will ask Dr. Cha, what is the most recent act of terrorism other than continuing to hold these hostages committed by the North Korean regime?

Mr. CHA. I would focus on cyber. The attack against Sony Pictures Entertainment.

Mr. SHERMAN. Yeah. I haven't studied the statute, but is that something that justifies designating a state as a state sponsor of terrorism?

Mr. CHA. I think it does. I mean, the administration defined it as cyber vandalism, I think, or cybercrime, but there was the destruction of hardware. There was a taking of information.

Mr. SHERMAN. Okay. So it is a strong legal argument whether you look at kidnapping movie actors and directors, or vandalizing movie software.

But now let's look at the policy. Is it good policy to designate North Korea as a state sponsor of terrorism? Does that move us in the direction of limiting this regime?

Mr. Albright.

Mr. ALBRIGHT. I think it is useful to consider. I mean, it was a big goal of theirs to be taken off the list. So it certainly argues to threaten to put them back on. I mean, again, I don't know the legal aspect of this and whether cyber attack is terrorism.

Mr. SHERMAN. Mr. Klingner and Dr. Terry.

Mr. KLINGNER. I think if you look at 18 U.S. Code section 2331 and the definitions there of what constitutes international terrorism, I think the Sony hack and the threats of "9/11-style attacks" against a population, and these threats were to intimidate and coerce a population, influence a policy of government, et cetera; I think that in and of itself fulfills it.

In my testimony in January, I included a list of other acts that they have done, including attempts against——

Mr. SHERMAN. Good. So that is in our record. And, Dr. Terry, would designating them be good foreign policy. I will ask for a quick answer.

Ms. TERRY. Yes. I absolutely agree. I think it would be largely symbolic, to be honest, but North Korea was very keen on getting off that list, as Victor knows. They tried very hard. It truly bothered them, so I think it is useful. I think it is a leverage that we can use against North Korea, and I do think they have done a lot of things, including repeated assassination attempts and kidnapping attempts on humans. So there is a whole list of reasons why they can be put back on the list.

Mr. SHERMAN. Just to conclude, I think we need to bring a lot more effort and settle for a much smaller objective. We have been trying to see a completely nonnuclear North Korea and somehow achieve that without doing anything that ruffled anybody's feathers, here or Beijing. What we ought to be is settling for less and being willing to ruffle some feathers to get even that limited objective. We should be willing to tax Chinese exports to the United

States. We should be willing to build the Voice of America towers. We should be willing to list them as a state sponsor of terrorism. They need a hell of a lot more carrots and a hell of a lot more sticks if we are even going to get them to something that most of you would say would be an unacceptable solution.

It is just much better than what is likely to happen if we do nothing. I yield back.

Mr. SALMON. Thank you.

Mr. Connolly.

Mr. CONNOLLY. Thank you, Mr. Chairman, and thank you all for being here. I come here as a member of this committee and subcommittee and also as the co-chair of the Congressional Caucus on Korea.

Let me begin by expressing my skepticism about the efficacy of sanctions. Up here, when we want to condemn, cite, punish bad behavior, almost always we invoke sanctions as if, well, that will deter the behavior. And I don't know—a former colleague of yours, Dr. Cha, Gary Hufbauer, wrote a very thoughtful book years ago on the history of sanctions and how effective they are and raised a lot of questions. You know, in some cases, they seemed to have had the desired effect, but usually, it is combined with some other external thing so that at the margins, whoops, the sanctions really made it hurt—oil prices plummeting or whatever it may be.

In and of themselves, it is very difficult to create a regime that really can squeeze to the point where we get the desired outcome and the intended target—you know, it renounces its undesirable behavior.

And I am just concerned here that, with respect to North Korea, I don't think we have—I mean, it is not apparent to me that we have a lot of options. I have noticed, for example, in the printed media now we are talking now about, well, maybe we can try to get countries to send back North Korean workers to deny North Korea that capital, that foreign exchange.

You mentioned, Dr. Cha, well, maybe we could target leadership through certain sanctions. So Kim Jong-un can't, you know, access Courvoisier. His father seemed to like Courvoisier, as I recall. But if we are reduced to that, just how effective, I mean, shouldn't we be realistic about what sanctions can and cannot do? And it just seems to me that we are, remember, the goal here is to give up that nuclear ambition and destroy those existing 15 nuclear weapons or whatever number. I mean, that is our goal. It may or may not be achievable, but what sanction provides that tradeoff, from the North Korean point of view?

Mr. CHA. Well, I have no disagreement with you, Congressman, about the inefficacy of sanctions thus far. I think where the policy debate really is, is that lack of efficacy because sanctions in general don't work or because we haven't done enough? And for many in the policy community, and I think for this administration, the answer right now is we haven't done enough because when we compare the sanctions on DPRK versus those on Iran, the Iran sanctions were much more comprehensive than what we are seeing on DPRK. So I think that is where the administration is now and that is where they have been pushing.

57

Having said that, I would agree with you. I mean, I think the sanctions are meant to do one of three things, and none of them are happening. They are supposed to either bring the North back to the table, which they haven't done. They are supposed to retard the growth of the program, which it hasn't done. Or, it is supposed to destabilize the regime. And it hasn't done any of these three things.

Mr. CONNOLLY. I will just say, when I commended Gary Hufbauer's book, that was pre-North Korea sanctions, I think, and he really raised a broader question, not about these sanctions with this regime, but sanctions in general. What kind of foreign policy really are sanctions? And they are of dubious value. I mean, sometimes they seem to have helped, but it is not clear you can single them out and say: That was dispositive. Rhodesia comes to mind.

Mr. ALBRIGHT. Can I add one?

Mr. CONNOLLY. Yes, and then we have got to go because we have got votes.

Mr. KLINGNER. There is a difference between sanctions and targeted financial measures. And the smart sanctions that have been done in the last 10 years are very different from what traditional trade sanctions have been. And a book I would commend would be ''Treasury's War,'' by Juan Zarate, a former Treasury Department official, which articulates the very strong differences.

You know, it is only this year that we actually have as many North Korean entities being sanctioned as Zimbabwe entities. So it took a number of years just to get to the level of Zimbabwe. And then, on the efficacy of diplomacy, some would say, well, North Korea builds nuclear weapons when we are not talking to them. That is true. They also build nuclear weapons when we are talking to them, and they also build nuclear weapons when they sign agreements never to build nuclear weapons and when they promise to give up the weapons that they promised never to build in the first place. We have had four agreements where they would never build weapons and four to give up those weapons, including the Leap Day agreement, which was a very low bar, and they broke that one.

Mr. ALBRIGHT. You know, I would just add, in the nuclear area, sanctions have——

Mr. SALMON. We have 4 minutes before we have to vote.

Mr. ALBRIGHT. Okay. I would just say, I think sanctions can work in the nuclear area better. But you can't do it alone. And I would agree with you. You have to have more.

Mr. SALMON. I thank the panel. I thank the committee members and appreciate all of the insight.

This meeting is adjourned, thank you.

[Whereupon, at 4:44 p.m., the subcommittee was adjourned.]

APPENDIX

SUBCOMMITTEE HEARING NOTICE
COMMITTEE ON FOREIGN AFFAIRS
U.S. HOUSE OF REPRESENTATIVES
WASHINGTON, DC 20515-6128

Subcommittee on Asia and the Pacific
Matt Salmon (R-AZ), Chairman

September 14, 2016

TO: MEMBERS OF THE COMMITTEE ON FOREIGN AFFAIRS

You are respectfully requested to attend an OPEN hearing of the Committee on Foreign Affairs, to be held by the Subcommittee on Asia and the Pacific in Room 2255 of the Rayburn House Office Building (and available live on the Committee website at http://www.ForeignAffairs.house.gov):

DATE: Wednesday, September 14, 2016

TIME: 3:00 p.m.

SUBJECT: North Korea's Perpetual Provocations: Another Dangerous, Escalatory Nuclear Test

WITNESSES: Victor Cha, Ph.D.
                  Senior Adviser and Korea Chair
                  Center for Strategic and International Studies

                  Mr. Bruce Klingner
                  Senior Research Fellow for Northeast Asia
                  The Heritage Foundation

                  Sue Mi Terry, Ph.D.
                  Managing Director
                  Bower Group Asia

                  Mr. David Albright
                  President and Founder
                  Institute for Science and International Security

By Direction of the Chairman

COMMITTEE ON FOREIGN AFFAIRS

MINUTES OF SUBCOMMITTEE ON _____ *Asia and the Pacific* _____ HEARING

Day__*Wednesday*__Date___*September 14*___Room_____*2172*_____

Starting Time ___*3:21pm*___ Ending Time ___*4:44pm*___

Recesses [____] (___to___) (___to___) (___to___) (___to___) (___to___) (___to___)

Presiding Member(s)

Salmon

Check all of the following that apply:

Open Session [✓]   Electronically Recorded (taped) [ ]
Executive (closed) Session [ ]   Stenographic Record [ ]
Televised [ ]

TITLE OF HEARING:

North Korea's Perpetual Provocations: Another Dangerous, Escalatory Nuclear Test

SUBCOMMITTEE MEMBERS PRESENT:

Perry, Duncan, Chabot
Bera, Meng, Lowenthal, Gabbard

NON-SUBCOMMITTEE MEMBERS PRESENT: *(Mark with an * if they are not members of full committee.)*

HEARING WITNESSES: Same as meeting notice attached? Yes [✓] No [ ]
(If "no", please list below and include title, agency, department, or organization.)

STATEMENTS FOR THE RECORD: *(List any statements submitted for the record.)*

TIME SCHEDULED TO RECONVENE _____
or
TIME ADJOURNED ___*4:44pm*___

Subcommittee Staff Associate

Foundation for Resilient Societies
52 Technology Way
Nashua NH 03060
www.resilientsocieties.org

June 28, 2013

President Barack Obama
The White House
1600 Pennsylvania Avenue NW
Washington, DC 20500

Subject: Government Emergency Actions on Electromagnetic Pulse Threats

Dear Mr. President:

We are writing to urge protection of the United States against both man-made and naturally-occurring electromagnetic pulse (EMP). The recent actions of Iran and North Korea—including ongoing nuclear weapons development and missile tests—increase the chance that these nations will threaten and perhaps even execute a high altitude nuclear EMP attack against the continental United States. However, if Presidential initiatives were to protect even a modest proportion of the U.S. electric power grid against EMP, nuclear deterrence could be strengthened and benefits to nuclear proliferators diminished.

The Commission to Assess the Threat to the United States from Electromagnetic Pulse Attack was authorized by the U.S. Congress and worked from 2001 to 2008 to conduct the most comprehensive study to date on EMP protection for civilian infrastructure. We ask the current Administration to revisit and implement selected findings of the EMP Commission. A summary of the EMP Commission findings on protection of electric power infrastructure is included as Appendix 1 to this letter. (Dr. William Graham, chairman of the EMP Commission, is both a director of our Foundation and a signatory to this letter.) Other government bodies also recommending EMP protection include the National Academy of Sciences and the National Intelligence Council.

We commend the Administration for supporting bipartisan efforts to protect against naturally-occurring EMP—also called "solar storms" or "geomagnetic disturbance"—and appreciate the recent White House report, "Space Weather Observing Systems: Current Capabilities and Requirements For The Next Decade." We also appreciate the positive ruling of the Nuclear Regulatory Commission (NRC) on Petition for Rulemaking PRM-50-96, a petition submitted by our Foundation which would require unattended backup power systems at nuclear power plants vulnerable to solar storm EMP. (See 77 Fed. Reg. 74788-74798; Dec 18, 2012 and Appendix 7 of this letter.) As the events at Fukushima amply showed, nuclear power plants without grid power—and without reliable and protected control and backup systems—can pose a catastrophic danger to surrounding populations. Without power to control and cool reactor cores and spent fuel pools, thousands of square miles surrounding scores of nuclear power plants in this country could be uninhabitable for centuries in the wake of a national-level EMP event. Additional reports of the EMP Commission are available to authorized persons through the Congress and the Department of Defense.

A high altitude nuclear EMP attack from North Korea is an imminent threat to the United States, and an EMP attack from Iran could shortly become an imminent threat. We propose three protective actions against rogue nations with nuclear EMP capability. In the short term, we propose emergency deployment of cost-effective missile defense systems, including Aegis systems that can defend against southern approaches to the continental United States; this proposal is more fully explained in Appendix 2. In the medium term, we propose E1 (fast pulse) protection of electric grid control rooms at regional balancing authorities, as well as E1 and E3 (magnetohydrodynamic pulse) protection of critical Extra High Voltage (EHV) transformers. This protection, while incomplete, would increase the uncertainty of a successful nuclear EMP attack and could have substantial deterrent effect upon rogue state adversaries. In the long-term, we propose that all high-priority critical infrastructures when upgraded or replaced should be subject to nuclear EMP protection standards; for example, all of the Bulk Power System under jurisdiction of FERC should eventually have both E1 and E3 protection.

Engineering practices for EMP protection are well developed and have been successfully implemented by the Department of Defense (DoD) for its strategic systems. The American public deserves protection for critical civilian infrastructure as well. It is particularly important for DoD to make its expertise available to the Department of Homeland Security, the Department of Energy, NRC, FERC, and the electric power industry. A summary of DoD expertise that could be used to provide EMP protection for the U.S. electric power grid is provided in Appendix 3.

While FERC has a standard for solar storm EMP protection in development, the timeline for installation of protective hardware will be in year 2015 at the earliest. In the meantime, and during the peak and active backside of the 11-year solar cycle, the United States will be unprotected, absent a government emergency plan to de-energize the electric grid upon warning of a severe solar storm. De-energizing transformers with long replacement times could reduce grid recovery time and save millions of lives.

Our legal analysis indicates that the President has existing authority to de-energize substantial portions of the three U.S. regional grid interconnections, including all nuclear, gas-fired, and oil-fired generation facilities. We understand from the NOAA Space Weather Prediction Center that a final 10 to 20-minute warning from the ACE satellite, as well as preliminary two-day warnings from space satellites closer to the sun, could be part of a feasible plan to de-energize vulnerable equipment within the electric grid. While the final warning time would be short, de-energizing the most vulnerable portions of the U.S. electric grid could still be accomplished if an emergency plan had previously been developed and all necessary processes and procedures were in place. Significantly, Presidential authority to de-energize critical generation facilities is non-delegable, except for nuclear power plants where the NRC has direct authority. More background on an emergency plan to de-energize generation facilities is explained in Appendix 4 of this letter; a review of Presidential legal authority is presented in Appendix 5.

In the fall of 2012 our Foundation conducted a pilot qualitative survey of national security and foreign policy experts regarding awareness of EMP threats. To our surprise, we found that EMP threats are poorly understood and often discounted among these experts, despite nuclear EMP protection being required for U.S. strategic defense systems and continuity of government for more than 40 years. Some in Washington view EMP as a problem without a ready solution and therefore politically infeasible to address. In actuality, Idaho National Laboratory has already tested a neutral blocking device to protect transformers against both nuclear E3 and severe solar storms. This blocking device is commercially available for a cost of $250,000 per substation. Furthermore, at least one electric utility (Centerpoint Energy in Houston, Texas) has installed on its own initiative a nuclear E1 hardened control room at a cost of $8.75 million dollars. Nations such as Israel are already implementing cost-effective EMP protection for their electric grids.

Focused EMP protection of the most critical infrastructure would be both practical and cost-effective. But lack of timely EMP protection could result in the death of over one hundred million Americans and threaten the existence of the United States as a functioning country.

There is increasing public awareness and concern over EMP threats. This legitimate public concern, if not addressed, could have a destabilizing effect on our society. Already there is a "prepper" movement, where individual citizens store food and water and sometimes take more extreme measures. But no amount of personal preparation can supplant the constitutional duty of the federal government to provide for a common defense. We urge the Administration to take concrete steps for EMP protection before the next major solar storm and before the Islamic Republic of Iran conducts a successful nuclear test. Actions for EMP protection must be made public—secret plans will not reassure the populace, nor will secret EMP defenses deter rogue nations.

Given the importance and immediacy of EMP threats to the United States and its population, we ask for the courtesy of a reply from the Administration. Thank you for consideration of our concerns.

Sincerely,

William R. Graham

Dr. William R. Graham, Chair of Congressional EMP Commission and former Assistant to the President for Science and Technology

[signature]

Ambassador Henry F. Cooper, former Director of the Strategic Defense Initiative Organization

[signature]

Dr. George H. Baker, Professor Emeritus, James Madison University

65

William R. Harris, International Lawyer & Secretary, Foundation for Resilient Societies

Stephen L. Mott, Nuclear Engineer; 30 years' experience in the nuclear power industry

Thomas S. Popik, Chairman, Foundation for Resilient Societies

Attachments:
Appendix 1: Extracts from Executive Report of Commission to Assess the Threat to the United States from Electromagnetic Pulse Attack
Appendix 2: An Immediate Plan to Defend U.S. against Nuclear EMP Attack
Appendix 3: EMP/GMD Protection of the U.S. Electric Power Grid
Appendix 4: Presidential Plan to Protect from Long-Term Electric Grid Outage Due to GMD
Appendix 5: Legal Authority for the President of the United States to Order Interruption of U.S. Electric Generation and Related Electric Grid Protections during a Severe Solar Geomagnetic Storm
Appendix 6: Recognizing Electromagnetic Pulse Attack
Appendix 7: Vulnerability of Nuclear Power Plants to Electromagnetic Pulse

cc:
The White House
Sylvia Mathews Burwell, Director, Office of Management and Budget
John P. Holdren, Director, Office of Science and Technology Policy
Lisa O. Monaco, Assistant to the President for Homeland Security and Counterterrorism
Susan E. Rice, Assistant to the President for National Security Affairs

Departments
Charles T. Hagel, Secretary of Defense
John F. Kerry, Secretary of State
Ernest J. Moniz, Secretary of Energy
Janet Napolitano, Secretary of Homeland Security

Agencies
James R. Clapper, Director of National Intelligence
Allison M. Macfarlane, Chairman, Nuclear Regulatory Commission
Kathryn Sullivan, Acting NOAA Administrator
Jon Wellinghoff, Chairman, Federal Energy Regulatory Commission

Appendix 1

Extracts from Executive Report of Commission to Assess the Threat to the United States from Electromagnetic Pulse Attack

Full report available at http://www.empcommission.org/docs/empc_exec_rpt.pdf.

ABSTRACT

Several potential adversaries have or can acquire the capability to attack the United States with a high-altitude nuclear weapon-generated electromagnetic pulse (EMP). A determined adversary can achieve an EMP attack capability without having a high level of sophistication.

EMP is one of a small number of threats that can hold our society at risk of catastrophic consequences. EMP will cover the wide geographic region within line of sight to the nuclear weapon. It has the capability to produce significant damage to critical infrastructures and thus to the very fabric of US society, as well as to the ability of the US and Western nations to project influence and military power.

The common element that can produce such an impact from EMP is primarily electronics, so pervasive in all aspects of our society and military, coupled through critical infrastructures. Our vulnerability is increasing daily as our use of and dependence on electronics continues to grow. The impact of EMP is asymmetric in relation to potential protagonists who are not as dependent on modern electronics.

The current vulnerability of our critical infrastructures can both invite and reward attack if not corrected. Correction is feasible and well within the Nation's means and resources to accomplish.

North Korea's Perpetual Provocations: Another Dangerous, Escalatory Nuclear Test
Subcommittee on Asia and the Pacific
House Committee on Foreign Affairs
Wednesday, September 14, 2016, 3:00 p.m.
Statement for the Record from Rep. Grace Meng

Chairman Salmon, Ranking Member Sherman, thank you for convening this timely hearing today and I would also like to thank our distinguished witnesses for joining us, some of you who joined us earlier this year in January after North Korea's fourth nuclear test. Welcome back, it's always nice to see familiar faces despite the circumstances.

The issue of North Korea's nuclear development has become a perennial topic that all too often becomes sidelined and forgotten. The dance has become all too familiar for us. North Korea tests a nuclear weapon, the international community condemns, a strongly worded statement comes out, sanctions follow, and then nothing. North Korea continues without changing its policy and here we are again after the fourth nuclear test.

This year alone, in the span of 8 months, North Korea has conducted two nuclear tests. Evidence from North Korea's fifth nuclear test indicates the yield could range anywhere from 10-20 kilotons. In other words, North Korea's nuclear weapons are approaching the size of the bomb used on Hiroshima in World War Two. To make matters worse, North Korea is also developing an array of different delivery vehicles for their nuclear weapons. Under Kim Jong-un's leadership, North Korea has conducted 37 missile tests, including a submarine launch ballistic missile (SLBM) capability.

North Korea's nuclear and missile development is a clear and present danger. What more can be done to support the Republic of Korea and Japan? What options do we have at our disposal to compel North Korea's behavior to change? This hearing is timely and I hope we find some solutions that will force North Korea back to the negotiating table and denuclearize.